Nuggets of Nevada County History

Nuggets of Nevada

 Juanita

NEVADA COUNTY HISTORICAL SOCIETY

MIDDLE FORK YUBA RIVER

English Dam

Welber Lake

LITTLE TRUKEE

TRUCKEE RIVER

SOUTH FORK YUBA

RIVER

Independence Lake

Boca

Floriston

Soda Springs

Donner Lake

Omega

BEAR RIVER

Truckee

TRUCKEE RIVER

Lake Tahoe

┼┼┼┼┼┼┼ Nevada County Narrow Gauge R R
─·─·─·─ County Boundary
⌇⌇⌇⌇⌇ Rivers & Streams

County History

Kennedy Browne

NEVADA CITY ⌘ CALIFORNIA

FIRST EDITION
LIMITED TO 2000 NUMBERED COPIES
Number *1533*

Cover Illustrations: Emma Nevada (Courtesy of California
State Library). Cornish Miner (Courtesy of Empire Mine State
Historic Park).

Library of Congress Catalog Card Number 83-23781

ISBN 0-915641-00-3

This book is dedicated to Nevada County for having such an interesting history, to the Nevada County Historical Society and Board of Directors for supporting me in writing about that history, and to Pete Browne, my "gentle critic," for giving me encouragement and support, for believing in me and the book, and for doing whatever needed to be done to see that what he believed in came through.

Juanita Kennedy Browne

My Thanks to

all the members and directors of the Nevada County Historical Society, the personnel of the Nevada County Libraries, and the volunteers in the Searls Historical Library for their pleasant and prompt help whenever asked.

My thanks, also, to everyone who loaned me photographs, material, and books or gave me advice, criticism, encouragement, and help including (but not limited to): Frances and John Burton, Madelyn Helling, Ed Tyson, Steve Green, Peter van der Pas, Pat Jones, Bob Paine, Margaret Trivelpiece, Ardis Comstock, Dorothy McMaster, Tom Macaulay, June McIntosh, Scott Browne, and Beryl Dick.

My special thanks goes to David Comstock, my knight in a jump suit, who led me safely through the labyrinth of getting this book from my word processor through the final details of design and publication.

And to Pete, my husband, my friend.

Contents

List of Illustrations

Unless otherwise noted, all photographs are courtesy of the Nevada County Historical Society's Searls Historical Library.

Introduction

When people think of Nevada County, they usually think of Gold! and the early 49ers who rushed to the area dreaming of quickly plucking out a fortune in gold nuggets and returning home wealthy. A few did, but most didn't. And that was just a short, small part of the history of Nevada County.

Although gold eventually earned Nevada County the title of being the largest, richest, and longest operating gold-quartz mining area in California, other resources, events, and personalities are bright facets in the rich history of the area. *Nuggets of Nevada County History* highlights some of the lesser known as well as some of the better known facets that are interesting, important, or entertaining.

In this book, anecdotes on how Humbug, Red Dog, Rough and Ready, and You Bet got their unusual names are mixed with information on various gold mining methods, the development of the Empire mine, one of the largest hard-rock mines in the world, and the events that led to the end of hydraulic mining.

The well-known, fabulous, eccentric Lola Montez shares the spotlight with the long-time child star Lotta Crabtree, the world-renowned soprano Emma Nevada, pioneer aviator Lyman Gilmore, Jr., and "The Never Come, Never Go," Nevada County's beloved narrow gauge railroad.

Truckee, a rough and wooly railroad-lumber camp in the high Sierra that gained respect through her butter, beer, and natural ice industries and early historical winter sports carnivals is joined by her fruitful foothill neighbor Chicago Park.

Events that led to the beginning of the end of the Nisenan Indians are included along with how another Indian, John Rollin Ridge, wrote the first version of the enduring legend of Joaquin Murietta.

This history begins in 1848, dares to venture beyond the confines of 1880 (where historical publishers Thompson and West stopped and few have ventured beyond), and plunges recklessly right through 1899, when Nevada County and the world teetered on the verge of the twentieth century.

Placer gold miners in the gold-rush era (Courtesy of California State Library).

GOLD!
In the Beginning

Contrary to popular belief, gold was not first discovered by James Marshall at Sutter's sawmill in 1848. Gold was not only found but mined in California much earlier.

Mexicans discovered placer deposits in southeastern California in 1775 and again near the Spanish mission of San Fernando in 1812. A minor gold rush developed in 1842 when gold was discovered near the pueblo of Los Angeles. But the rush never became big, and the gold was soon worked out.

In 1846, Thomas O. Larkin, the consul at Monterey, officially notified U.S. Secretary of State James Buchanan of gold in California.

Despite these discoveries, the virulent gold fever lay dormant, and California remained a sparsely settled wilderness.

Then, on Monday morning, January 24, 1848, a shiny pebble caught Marshall's eye as he checked out the tailrace of Sutter's recently erected sawmill on the south fork of the American River. When Marshall bent over and picked up the pea-sized rock, he thought he had found gold, but the color didn't seem quite right. When the nugget flattened but didn't break when he beat it with a rock, Marshall was sure he had gold.

He picked up several other small pieces and yelled at the men working at the sawmill, "Boys, I believe I have found a gold mine!"

Did everyone whoop and holler, dash to the spot, and start digging like mad? No.

One of the boys answered, "I guess not."

Another added, "Oh, no. That can't be."

But J. S. Brown gave the rock a sort of taste test. He took a healthy bite and declared, "Gold, boys, gold."

Everyone fell to testing.

Mrs. Wimmer, the cook, who had lived in a gold mining region in Georgia, threw a piece in a boiling kettle of lye.

The blacksmith heated and pounded a nugget.

Their verdict? Gold!

But the gold fever still didn't erupt.

Henry Bigler made the following laconic note in his diary:

"Monday 24th. This day some kind of mettle was found in the tail race that looks like goald, first discovered by James Martial, the Boss of the Mill."

Marshall went to Sutter's Fort and told Sutter of the discovery. The metal was weighed and tested chemically and again declared to be gold. But Sutter refused to return to the sawmill right away because it was raining and he hadn't eaten his supper.

The next day Sutter rode to the sawmill and pledged everyone to keep the discovery a secret. Everyone said they would. But they didn't. Drip by drip, the news leaked out.

On March 15, 1848, the San Francisco *Californian* mentioned briefly that a gold mine had been found at Sutter's Mill and about $30 worth of gold had been received at New Helvetia (Sutter's Fort).

Soon after, in May 1848, the only other San Francisco paper, *The California Star,* declared that the gold mines were a "sham" and that anyone who went looking for gold was "superlatively silly."

Sam Brannan, the owner of *The California Star* and never one afraid of being silly, either mildly or superlatively if it would make him a fast buck, checked out the story of the sawmill and began to plan one of the greatest publicity stunts of the time.

Sam, part owner of a store at Fort Sutter, shrewdly foresaw the vast possibilities of selling supplies and equipment to eager prospectors passing by the Fort on their headlong rush to the long foretold El Dorado now quietly forming in Coloma Valley.

First, Sam bought up all the gold mining supplies he could find. Then, in May 1848, disheveled and bursting with enthusiasm, Sam tramped through the streets waving a quinine bottle filled with gold flakes and shouting for all San Francisco to hear and the world to echo, "Gold! Gold! Gold from the American River!"

That did it.

Gold fever quickly strangled San Francisco. Stores, fields, homes,

John A. Sutter (Courtesy of Darwin Publications).

and wives were deserted as the few hundred men in the area left for the gold fields.

Next, the fever swooped south. Soon, Monterey, Santa Barbara, Los Angeles, Santa Cruz, and San Diego were almost depopulated. Even the way from San Jose was crowded with gold-rushers.

The fever spread out from San Francisco in an ever-widening circle, slapped against all the shores of the world, and rushed inland.

Sailors jumped ship in San Francisco, soldiers deserted their posts, farmers left their cows, lovers their sweethearts, public officials their desks, and storekeepers their shops—except for Sam Brannan. He was making a fortune selling 20 cent gold pans for $16.

GOLD!
When, Where, and How They Found It

According to J. S. Hittell, an early California historian, most early gold deposits were discovered by accident by "poor and ignorant" men who would come upon gold sparkling in streams or in rock outcroppings while out walking or hunting.

A hunter in Tuolumne County spotted gold in a nearby rock while skinning a grizzly bear that he had shot.

In Mariposa County, a miner was attacked by a robber. Shots were exchanged and when a stray bullet hit a rock the keen-eyed miner noticed an interesting glitter. The miner quickly killed the robber and rushed to examine the rock, which proved to be—Gold!

A man hunting rabbits near Angel's Camp jammed his ramrod into the roots of a manzanita bush and turned up gold-bearing quartz. Using only the ramrod, he took out gold worth $700 in one day.

In Nevada County, two unsuccessful miners went on a drunken spree before leaving to seek better prospects. During their pre-departure celebration, they stumbled over a large boulder, which rolled down a steep hill, broke off a piece of jutting rock, and exposed a rich vein of gold. The jubilant miners decided their prospects were never better than right where they were.

According to several popular tales, other "poor but ignorant" and lucky miners in the Nevada County area also stumbled onto gold deposits. And having a cow, ox, or cattle seemed to help.

Up near Downieville, an early miner claimed he found gold in a slaughtered cow's belly.

Placer gold miners in the gold-rush era (Courtesy of California State Library).

Way back in the late 1840s, herds of wandering cattle brought some of the first emigrants and settlers into the Grass Valley area where within a few years millions in gold were found laying around in creeks and crevices, streams and ravines.

Soon after, as one version of history goes, in June, October, or December of 1850 along came George Knight who stumbled across a rich gold-bearing quartz deposit on Gold Hill while out chasing his cow.

(Some sources say George's name was McKnight. Some say he didn't have a cow, and he only stubbed his toe. Another says he didn't even stub his toe.)

George's discovery didn't create much immediate excitement as most miners stuck to the better known and less expensive placer mining methods.

Then in October 1850, George Roberts bumped into another rich hard-rock ledge on Ophir Hill. This time the miners went wild and thousands filled the surrounding hills to stake out claims.

Roberts worked his ledge for a short time, pocketed his profits, and sold his claim. Some say that George sold his claim for the paltry sum of $350. That claim, located on one of the richest mineral veins in California, was the beginning of the Empire mine operation, which eventually became the oldest, biggest, and richest hard-rock mine in the area.

While out hunting his family cow, a Rough and Ready man stumbled over a beautiful kidney shaped nugget that assayed at over $1200.

Some historians also claim that it was while watching a neighbor try to shoo a cow out of his garden by hitting the cow in the face with water from a garden hose that L. A. Pelton perfected the concept of the Pelton wheel, which revolutionized the use of water power in hard-rock mining. Others say that the neighbor was just watering the garden and accidentally hit the cow. In a recent history of El Dorado County, it is claimed that Pelton either stole or simply took the idea of the Pelton wheel from an invention by Charles Green.

In 1880, a man in Dutch Flat picked up a rock to throw at his cow and discovered the rock contained $100 in gold.

Since similar stories are repeated again and again in place after place, the cow part of some of these tales might be partially bull.

But the stories persist, and some of them are apparently true.

Only a few years ago, in an unnamed Sierra meadow, a man kicked what he thought was a "cow pie" only to discover he had kicked up one of the largest gold nuggets found in recent history.

GOLD!
Getting It Out

The first prospectors who poured over California usually stopped just long enough to pick up a change of clothes, a couple of blankets, a pickax, trowel, spade, crowbar, sheath knife, and gold pan (maybe from Sam Brannan). Then off they'd rush with pick over shoulder and pan in hand to prospect along river beds and streams.

At the news of a new strike—miners seemed able to smell out a strike—hundreds would pick up their simple tools and converge on a single stream and rapidly pluck out the most visible and accessible placer gold.

However, placer mining involved more than just picking up big chunks of free gold or swishing a little gravel, dirt, and water around in a gold pan. It was hard, back-straining work. Digging, dumping, and washing yards of rock and dirt through gold-catching devices while standing knee deep in near-freezing water was not an easy way to seek a fortune.

A few placer miners did truly make "fabulous" strikes, but most would have done better financially if they had stayed at home. They would also have been much more comfortable.

As the bigger, richer, and more accessible gold deposits were worked and reworked with more and more men (and a smidgin of women) using bigger and bigger equipment, more and more heaps of dirt and more and more water had to be used to process out even a little pile of gold dust.

By 1853, the California gold rush was almost over. When the streams and rivers had seemingly been picked clean, disappointed

Coyote diggins.

miners began to move out of California to search for new mining frontiers or to return home—usually with little to show for all their time and trouble. They never knew that they had left behind large, rich placer deposits of gold suspended high overhead in the gravel of ancient riverbeds or locked in quartz-rock ledges and veins that extended for hundreds of miles underground.

In California, there are two types of gold deposits: placer and quartz.

In Nevada County, placer mining included first the mining of alluvial placer deposits where gold was mixed in with detritus (clay, silt, gravel, and sand) in live streams.

In this form of mining, water was used as a basic tool to wash the soil and gravel through gold pans, wooden bowls, Indian baskets, rockers, long toms, ground sluices, and sluice boxes.

Since gold is seven times as heavy as rock and gravel, the gold settles to the bottom of these devices where it is recovered after the worthless debris is washed away.

Placer deposits were also found in tertiary (prehistoric) river beds, now dry and frequently pushed upwards away from present-day streams. Gold in these deposits was mixed with gravel, which was sometimes cemented by geological pressure.

These gravel and cement placer deposits were first worked by digging shafts or drifts and later by hydraulicking.

Rich deposits of gold were also found in veins of quartz throughout the area. The hard-rock mining methods used to extract this type of gold deposit are complex and expensive, which, for a time, discouraged the development of this kind of mining.

But many miners in Nevada County chased the golden rainbow wherever it pointed.

As early as 1850, miners traced a streak of rich placer gold-bearing gravel to a high and dry hill near Nevada City. Immediately the siren song of "Gold!" pulled swarming masses who staked out small claims all over the hill. Since the richer deposits were below the surface, the problem was: how to get it out?

Well, if you've dug a well or dug a hole for an outhouse, you can dig a hole in the ground to get to pay dirt. And that is what they did.

The area was soon dotted with little holes. Beside these myriad of holes were mounds of pay dirt that had been hauled up by buckets on windlasses like water from a well and dumped. The dirt then had to be hauled in carts or in buckets down to Deer Creek to be washed and processed.

Because the area looked like so many coyote burrows, the place was appropriately named Coyoteville on Coyote Hill, and this placer mining method was called "coyoteing."

In the meantime, other miners who had discovered rich deposits of gold-bearing gravel or natural cement in areas remote from water had solved the problem of getting water to process the pay dirt in another manner. Instead of taking the dirt to the water, they brought the water to the dirt by digging first short then longer and longer water ditches or building long, elaborate wooden flume and pipe systems to divert water sources at higher elevations to feed by gravity to their "diggings."

According to most historians, around 1852, Anthony Chabot saved himself a lot of hard shovel-work by gravity-feeding a stream of water through a canvas hose to wash loose gravel into his sluice box. And by 1853, Edward E. Matteson had improved upon the idea. He added a nozzle—later called a monitor or giant—to a canvas hose, pointed the powerful stream of water under high pressure at the hillside, and quickly and efficiently washed it down into his sluice box.

Anthony (Antoine) Chabot.

News of the idea spread rapidly, and so began the hydraulic mining techniques in Nevada County, which soon stirred up a lot more than pay dirt.

In late 1850, other miners awakened to the richness of the gold-quartz deposits that George Knight and George Roberts had stumbled across and swarmed to those areas and staked out claims. In a short time they pounded out several million dollars worth of gold with the primitive hard-rock method of smacking the rock loose with a hammer and then grinding it up in a hand mortar to retrieve the gold.

As these surface outcroppings were worked out, miners were forced to devise more elaborate, costly, and sophisticated methods and machinery for getting the gold out of the deep rich veins that wandered hundreds of feet below the surface.

The inexperience of the miners, the crudeness of the early machinery, lack of capital, and poor management led to many disastrous hard-rock mining failures.

The miners had to learn how to blast out and timber tunnels as they inched their way down hard-rock veins.

How to break up the rock so the gold could be extracted presented another major problem. At first, crude stamp mills made from tree trunks covered with iron were used. Eventually, heavy iron stamp mills were manufactured. These stamp mills with iron pummeling tappets that could crush large quantities of ore were first powered by water and steam, then later, by electricity.

Some of the hardest problems were solved by tin and copper miners when they came from Cornwall, England to work in the mines and brought with them their invaluable skills and knowledge of hard-rock mining techniques and equipment.

With more and more experience, skill, knowledge, and capital investments, came first small then larger and larger success. In time, Nevada County became one of the most productive and longest operating hard-rock gold mining areas in the world.

And thereon rests much of Nevada County's continuing historical fame. However, a few other things were going on in the area besides mining.

Edward E. Matteson.

WHAT'S IN A NAME?

Grass Valley

What's in a name? Sometimes confusion and frustration.

What's so confusing about a simple name like Grass Valley, California?

Well, nothing now. But it wasn't always so simple.

The first white emigrants who passed through the area and let their cattle, oxen, and horses graze on the lush green pastureland referred to the area as the "grassy valley."

Then in September 1849, along came a small group from Boston who built cabins, opened a store, and settled near the ravine along Wolf Creek to prospect for gold. They, logically, dubbed this first settlement Boston Ravine.

Other settlers continued to use the original, more descriptive name of Grass Valley.

When later prospectors and settlers noted that Grass Valley lay about halfway between settlements that had sprung up in Rough and Ready and Nevada City, the business section along Main Street became known as Centreville.

In November 1850, a postal route was started between Nevada City and Marysville, and the post office was officially named Centreville. But the name didn't stick.

Consider the plight of the poor mailman who not only had to deliver the mail on a mule, but had to contend with delivering letters addressed to Boston Ravine, Grass Valley, Centreville, Grass Valley near Rough and Ready, and Centreville near Boston Ravine.

That's got to be both frustrating and confusing.

Grass Valley in 1852 (Courtesy of Dave Comstock).

Anyway, logic and sanity and popular opinion soon won out and the area was renamed Grass Valley.

Nevada City

The first settlement in what is now called Nevada City was made by miners, 49ers, in the area where Gold Run Creek and Deer Creek meet. Then in October 1849, A. B. Caldwell built a store where Trinity Episcopal Church is now located.

Since Caldwell had another store four miles down Deer Creek, the location of his second store became known as Caldwell's Upper Store. That's logical—except—the area was also called Deer Creek Dry Diggins.

Nevada City in 1852 (Courtesy of California State Library).

In March 1850, a government was established when Mr. Stamps was elected alcalde (an administrative office) and the citizens decided that the growing town needed an official and stable name. Among the names considered were: Sierra, Aurora, Nevada, Deer Creek, and Gold Run.

By popular decision, the name Nevada, meaning "snow covered" or "white as snow," was selected. But the "elite" sometimes called it Nevada City.

When the territory of Nevada (later to become the state of Nevada) was created in 1861 (over the loud protests of "our Nevada" citizens), "our Nevada"—to avoid further confusion—definitely became Nevada City—most of the time.

Rough and Ready

Hooray for Rough and Ready! From the beginning, this area, which was settled by rough and ready miners who were independent as all "get out," never went through a name change. Its character hasn't changed either.

In 1849, a small group of Eastern men, known as the Rough and Ready Company, arrived in what was eventually to become Nevada County and began poking around for gold.

Their leader, Captain A. A. Townsend, had named the company after Old Rough and Ready General Zachary Taylor, who in his Army career had waged brilliant campaigns against both Mexicans and Indians and had recently been elected the 12th President of the United States.

While out hunting for game, one of the company stooped for a drink of water and discovered a nice hunk of gold in a ravine. The company quickly moved into the area, staked out claims, built a few cabins, established a trading post, named the site Rough and Ready, and began hauling out placer gold at a good clip.

That was the beginning of a town that lived up to its name. A town that mushroomed in size and soon rivaled Nevada City and Grass Valley in population, prosperity, and tall tales.

The Rough and Ready miners were probably no more rough than anyone in the other nearby settlements, but they certainly were independent enough to change even their national allegiance whenever it suited their purpose.

This is how the popular story usually goes—whether it is a tall tale or true.

Rough and Ready in 1857 (Courtesy of Dave Comstock).

A cheating "slicker" strolled into Rough and Ready and made a crazy proposition to Joe Swiegart, a Rough and Ready miner. The "slicker" wanted to buy the miner's claim for a large sum of money, but he wanted to test the claim to make sure it was as rich as everyone claimed. This was the "slicker's" proposition: he would work the claim for a day. If he took out $200 or more in gold, he would give Joe the gold and buy the claim for the proposed price. If he failed to take out $200, he would keep what he dug out to pay for his labor and the deal for buying the claim was off.

Joe knew he had a rich claim, so he accepted the deal. He even insisted that they draw up a legally binding contract.

Bright and early the morning of the "test," the "slicker" went to work with a fury—for awhile. But as the amount of gold he was taking from the claim got closer and closer to $200, he worked slower and slower. When he had dug out about $180 worth of gold, he "flat out" quit, took the gold, and started to leave.

When Joe protested, the "slicker" claimed he didn't say he would work a whole day.

In a fury, Joe proposed to his friends that they string the cheating rascal up. Most of the miners thought that was a good way to settle the dispute. But a few objected and pointed out that the "slicker" had actually done nothing illegal according to the contract—dirty, perhaps, but not downright illegal. Besides, he was a U.S. citizen and they couldn't just string him up or even run him out of town like they could Indians, Mexicans, and other "foreigners."

Well, Joe and his backers had a rough and ready solution: secede from the Union and organize an independent government and make their own laws.

And secede they did, on April 7, 1850. Then they took back the gold from the "slicker" and ran the rascal out of their newly independent Great Republic of Rough and Ready.

As the Fourth of July drew nearer and nearer—the first for the new state of California and a great day for knocking off work and tanking up on "tanglefoot whiskey"—members of the Great Republic suddenly realized they couldn't join the celebration as they were no longer members of the great U. S. of A. So, by mass consent, Rough and Ready immediately rejoined the Union.

Washington D.C. never knew what they had won or lost.

And that's why the world-renowned Rough and Ready Secession Day celebration, which is held each year on the last Sunday of June, came into being many years later.

Why in June instead of April? Because citizens of the town are still as independent as all "get out."

The proof? They took on the U.S. post office and won.

During World War II, the Rough and Ready post office was discontinued for about five years. When citizens reapplied for a post office, officials replied they could not have two names. They could be Rough or they could be Ready, but they could not be Rough and Ready.

Local citizens stood their ground and said it would be Rough and Ready or nothing. In 1948, the post office officials gave in, and Rough and Ready it has been ever since.

Nevada County

When the early 48ers and later 49ers were pouring into this area naming everything like Adam in the Garden of Eden, California was not a state but a territory that had been ceded to the U.S. by Mexico in the Treaty of Guadalupe Hidalgo in 1848.

On February 18, 1850, to establish some semblance of government and law and order in the vast and sparsely settled but rapidly filling territory, California was split into 27 counties. Gigantic Yuba

County included present-day Yuba, Sierra, Nevada, and parts of Placer Counties. Marysville was the county seat.

After long congressional debates as to whether California should be admitted as a free or slave state, California was finally admitted to the U.S. as a free state on September 9, 1850.

In the meantime, "locals" complained that the county government in Marysville was too far away to be of any use and that the only county official who ever visited this area was the tax assessor followed closely by the tax collector, the last government officials anyone wanted to see.

The California Legislature eventually awakened to the problems of governing such a large area of widely scattered settlements; and on April 25, 1851, county boundaries were redrawn and Nevada County was formed with Nevada City as the county seat.

Humbug???

If you're an Irishman at heart on St. Patrick's Day and believe in leprechauns and hidden pots of gold, you'll probably believe this story, too.

Two Irishmen and a German found a rich deposit of gold in a remote creek in 1851.

When they ran low on supplies, one of the Irishmen went into Nevada City. His partners had cautioned him, repeatedly, to keep the location of their hidden pot of gold a secret.

While buying provisions, his lips were sealed. As he loaded his provisions onto his mule, his lips were sealed. Bystanders became "curiouser and curiouser" at his un-Irish-like taciturnness, and their interest soared when he paid for his supplies from a rich "poke" of gold.

Then like a true Son of Erin, the Irishman opened his mouth just enough to pack away a good supply of Irish whiskey, and he began to boast of his rich strike. But like a wily leprechaun, he refused to reveal the location of his pot of gold.

When he had finished his business and headed his mule out of town, a train of gold-seekers followed stealthily behind until he arrived at his campsite.

The horde of miners spread out and panned up and down the creek. They found nothing; and, one by one, they left declaring disgustedly, "Humbug! All Humbug!" And that is how the creek and a later settlement got their names.

When the settlement applied for a post office, the postal department decided that California was already too full of "Humbugs," so the settlement, not the creek, was officially renamed North Bloomfield in 1857. And that's no humbug.

Little York Township

In April 1852, Nevada County was divided into seven townships: Nevada, Grass Valley, Rough and Ready, Bridgeport, Grizzly Bear, Eureka, and Bear River. One month later, an eighth township, Little York, was created out of portions of the Grass Valley and Bear River townships.

Although miners first settled on the ridge between Bear River and Steephollow Creek in 1849, no one paid much attention until 1852 when trampling troops rushed in after hearing rumors of rich strikes.

A town was laid out and free lots were available for the claiming. The only rule was that you not build your shack in the middle of the laid-out streets.

By the spring of 1852, hundreds of miners and merchants had claimed lots and built homes, stores, hotels, saloons, and shops.

Then things got complicated.

Some of the miners were from the East, and some were from the West. Here the "twains" did meet, and they disagreed.

The Eastern men wanted to name the new mining metropolis Little York. The Western men preferred St. Louis. The Easterners won, and the town and the township became Little York.

In June 1878, a fire (which was believed to be incendiary because the water hose had been chopped into tiny pieces) reached the powder house of the Little York Company and 1400 pounds of giant powder exploded with a roar, "knocked things endwise," and blew most of Little York off the map.

Red Dog

Historians and storytellers tell different versions as to how the mining town of Red Dog got its name.

Most historians agree that the area was named after a mining district in Illinois.

A. A. Sargent, early newspaper editor, historian, lawyer, politician, diplomat, and storyteller, claimed the town was named after a

Residence and mine of John Hussey near Red Dog (Courtesy of Darwin Publications).

miner with long red hair who could usually be found lying drunk in the streets.

A more romantic version is that early miners were often awakened in the middle of the night by a giant, red, howling dog that was sometimes accompanied by a wild, beautiful girl in tattered, scanty clothing. The miners, showing more sense than usual, named the town after the red dog and not something like Wild Girl or Girl and Dog.

After a time, the sleep-shattering pair disappeared.

Many years later, a veiled woman got off the stage and checked into a run-down Red Dog hotel.

One night a young boy along with his red dog discovered the mysterious woman standing on a hill silhouetted in the moonlight with a jaunty tam-o'shanter perched on her head. The boy's dog rushed to her and set up a din that awakened the old timers and reminded them of the old howling Red Dog days.

As Red Dog grew and prospered, some citizens in a town meeting in July 1852—either seeking more sophistication or trying to keep up with the name changes of other settlements—wanted to change

The Red Dog Odd Fellows' hall after removal to You Bet.

the name to Brooklyn. The opposition preferred the name of Chalk Bluff.

Once again post office officials stepped in and "clarified" the matter. Brooklyn had been spoken for in Alameda County. Since two towns can't have the same name in the same state, the town remained Red Dog.

As happened so often in those early mining days, in August 1862, a fire wiped out the entire business district of Red Dog and many of the homes. But since the mines were doing well, the town was quickly rebuilt, bigger and better than ever.

Ironically, while it was fire that blew Little York off the map, it was water that washed up Red Dog.

During the winter of 1867–68, more than 100 days of continuous rain washed away hydraulic ditches and flumes, destroyed the water supply that was essential for working the mines, and buried mining equipment and rich "pay dirt" under tons of mud and debris. Thousands of dollars of investments were lost. Most of the miners and merchants left the area. A few tore down their buildings and moved them about a mile over to You Bet.

In the summer of 1870, some of the members of the Odd Fellows' lodge came back and moved their lodge to You Bet.

Today, all that remains of Red Dog is the name, a few tall tales, and a cemetery.

Walloupa

Walloupa, which was also born in the Little York township mining excitement of 1852, lived but a short time.

When miners swarmed to the spot, the town was named Walloupa after a chief in Wema's band of Indians.

About 400 miners and businessmen hastily built the usual necessities of houses, saloons, and stores. The town and businesses thrived for a few months until miners scampered away first to Red Dog then on to You Bet at the word of richer strikes in those areas.

By 1860, the remains of Walloupa had also been transplanted to You Bet.

Gouge Eye

In 1855, a group of French miners staked out a claim. Then along came another company of miners and jumped the claim. In the battle that followed, a Frenchman's eye was gouged out.

Later, when a rich lead was discovered on Hunt's Hill in the same area, the mining camp became known as both Hunt's Hill and Gouge Eye.

Not to be left behind by their neighbors in selecting more civilized town names, the citizens once tried to change the name to Camden, but it didn't take.

In 1857, history repeated itself when during a brawl at a Gouge Eye Christmas ball, a combatant's eye was gouged out.

By 1879, only a small combined store-and-saloon and a few houses remained. Gouge Eye was soon gone.

You Bet

I wouldn't bet on the popular story of how You Bet got its name.

Around 1857, Lazarus Beard built a small saloon, 12 x 12 feet, on a hill opposite Walloupa. When people from Walloupa wanted to rest and relax, they'd come up the hill to Beard's saloon.

Business was so good, Beard decided to expand and become a town. But he couldn't think of a name.

Beard would often consult with his steady customers, William King and James Toddkill, from Walloupa. Beard would supply them with whiskey to keep their brains working and the good names rolling. Since they liked their job and especially their pay, they would suggest names they were sure Beard would reject.

Beard had a favorite expression, which was—you guessed it—"You bet."

One day the namepickers crossed themselves up when they suggested that Beard name his settlement You Bet. His answer? "You Bet!"

You Bet it became, and the name-seekers had worked out their free liquor lode.

By 1860, most of the people from Walloupa had moved over to You Bet, which by 1864 was a prospering town surrounded by many mining operations. Later, residents from Red Dog also moved in. But as with other mining towns in the Little York township, when the mines were worked out, the miners left for richer fields, and by the late 1930s You Bet had gradually disappeared.

The Beginning of the End of
THE NISENAN INDIANS

An old joke contends that the American Indians could have saved themselves a lot of trouble and pain if they had simply tightened their immigration laws. They should never have allowed white people into their country.

That was certainly true of the local Nisenan Indians—Southern Maidu—who were more affected by the gold rush than any other Indians in California because they were smack dab in the middle of the most productive portions of the gold country.

The native Indians soon discovered that the Americans had "taking ways." They took anything they wanted. And they believed that not only did they have a God-given right to all of California but to all the gold in California

In an effort to keep peace and order when California became a U.S. territory, native Indians were informed that they were to abide by laws laid down unilaterally by the U.S. government. They must look to the President of the U.S. as their "great father" who takes care of his "good children," and they must obey the Indian agents who acted under their "great father's" orders.

Among the laws laid down by the "great father" was the stipulation that any Indian caught stealing a horse was to be shot. If one was caught killing or stealing cattle, he was to be flogged—"well" but not "cruelly"—like any thief. Indians could bring complaints against white men, but these complaints would be settled by white authorities. And no white man could be convicted of a crime solely on the testimony of an Indian.

Furthermore, Indians employed by whites were supposed to carry a certificate of employment for identification, and "wild" or "unemployed" Indians were suppose to carry a "passport" when visiting white settlements.

U.S. troops were located along major emigration trails to keep the peace and be ready should trouble break out between the white emigrants and settlers and the Indians. One such outpost in this area was Camp Far West located near Johnson's crossing on the Bear River.

In general, the Nisenan Indians were peaceful and unwarlike. They were contemptuously called "Diggers" by the whites, because they dug and ate roots as a part of their diet of wild game, fish, bulbs, and roots.

Along with other Maidu chiefs, Chief Wema cautioned his people in this area to avoid the white gold-seekers as much as possible. Most of them did.

A few showed early prospectors like Jonas Spect where to prospect for gold. Unaware of the value of gold, except perhaps as nice heavy rocks to be used in bringing down small game with a sling, some Indians traded gold at Simmon Storms and David Bovyer's trading post in the Rough and Ready township for trinkets and beads at a huge profit to Bovyer and Storms.

Some Indians were employed to work gold claims. In exchange for their knowledge of where to find gold and their labor in extracting it, the Indians were generally given a few pieces of calico and some "indifferent" food.

The Indians who didn't cooperate or retreat were simply shoved aside. A few were killed. At times, prospectors shot up Indian villages just for target practice.

As more and more interloping whites poured into the area in 1849 and 1850, they scared away game and muddied fishing waters, which disrupted and destroyed the Indian's natural food supply.

As their food supply became more scarce, the Indians adapted new hunting techniques. Since the whites were taking gold, lumber, fish, land, and game without so much as a "by your leave," a few Indians began taking from the whites the food supplies and cattle they needed to survive.

The whites didn't think this was fair and called it "stealing." Trouble was bound to erupt, and it soon did. But it didn't take U.S. troops and white miners more than a few weeks to settle things— their way.

Simmon Storms (Courtesy of Peter S. Shearer).

In early May 1850, two Indians were shot and killed by some whites for allegedly stealing some cattle. Some reports contend that the cattle were later found.

In retaliation, a small party of Indians attacked the two Holt brothers, Samuel and George, at their sawmill outside of Grass Valley. Samuel was killed, and the sawmill was burned.

Although severely wounded, George fought his way to the nearby Walsh and Wheeler sawmill.

Chief Wema in a most brave, civilized, and conciliatory—or most foolish—act brought in the body of Samuel and turned it over to the whites.

In the meantime, Captain John Day went to Camp Far West and returned with a few soldiers who were joined by a large group of miners from Deer Creek. These armed forces quickly punished the Indians "most severely" and then chased them out of the area.

When Major General Thomas J. Green of the California Militia with the support of U.S. troops and volunteers jumped into the fray, they pursued the Indians even farther afield, trapped and killed some, and took some women and children hostage.

Green then sent a note to Chief Wema and other local chiefs telling them that if they wanted peace and their people back, they'd better come in and sign a treaty.

Although the Indians far outnumbered the whites at that time, they were not trained, organized, or equipped as warriors. While they were generally on foot and armed with only primitive bows and arrows, they were being pursued by organized bands of whites on horseback and armed with pistols and rifles.

Wema and the other Maidu chiefs had only two choices: accept the white man's terms or continue to run and eventually be caught and killed.

On May 25, 1850, Wema and Buckler (Bukla) and Poolel (Pulel) and some of their men came into the town of Kearney on the Bear River, made their marks, and agreed to abide by the white man's treaty. This was the beginning of the end of the Indians in this area.

Among other things, the treaty stipulated that any Indian who robbed, murdered, or offended any American citizen was to be turned in to American authorities for punishment. To prevent these friendly Indians from being mistaken for unfriendly Indians, they were not to carry arms while in or near white settlements.

In exchange, they were to be paid $1000 semiannually for ten years, if the U.S. government accepted the treaty. They were also to be allowed to work in the gold mines.

Green confided to his superiors that he believed the Indians would abide by the treaty. He also surmised that as the Indians would be content to work for "one-fourth the wages of the white men," they could be most useful to the miners.

Ironically, Congress refused to ratify the treaty. Instead, the papers were hidden in the Congressional Archives for years, and neither the public nor the Indians were informed that the treaty was invalid.

Another incident near Spenceville in the summer of 1851 brought quick retaliation against the Indians.

When a young lad traveling with a teamster dropped behind the wagon, he was shot and killed by two Indians.

A band of white men quickly organized and raided an Indian camp on the Yuba River and took a group of Indian prisoners back to Rough and Ready. Like in an old western movie, the miners were finally convinced that they had the wrong Indians as the murderers belonged to Wema's tribe. This was not the first nor last time irate whites in a hurry to see justice done grabbed the wrong Indians.

An angry and aggressive mob of whites charged into one of Wema's camps outside of Rough and Ready. Their belligerent attitudes so angered the Nisenans that they bravely stood up to the whites and drove them out.

Another posse was quickly raised and was charging back toward Wema's village when they met Wema, his son, and a small group of Indians. The Indians were covered with rifles and ordered to come along, and during the "parley" Wema agreed to turn in the accused.

Indian runners were sent out and in three days returned with two Indians. Judge Roberts questioned the Indians for about 15 hours. In the meantime, about 500 impatient miners picked their own jury and began their own investigation and trial.

Eventually, the Indian, Collo, was determined to be guilty, and the other Indian was turned loose. Collo confessed his guilt and named his accomplice who had left the country.

By now, the restless miners had decided to bring the whole issue to a hasty conclusion. One jumped up on a table and announced that Collo was to be hanged at ten in the morning.

Indian runners were instructed to go out and bring in all the Indians they could find to witness and heed this example of white man's justice. About 1000 Indians were gathered in.

A wagon was driven under a tree, and Collo was told to step up on a box, which he did coolly and bravely. A rope was thrown over a tree limb, the noose was adjusted around Collo's neck, the box was removed, and Collo was hanged.

Although the hanging was illegal, most of the whites felt it was "well-deserved," and the example did keep the peace for some time.

Bit by bit, the white men took away from the Nisenans what they valued more than gold: their land and their way of life. Time and again the whites promised the Indians food and protection in exchange for more and more land and more and more concessions. And time after time the whites failed to fulfill their part of the bargain. The Indians quickly learned not to believe the white man's promises, but they had no power to either negotiate or retaliate.

Under more orders and treaties from the "great white father" that the helpless Indians were forced to agree to, many of the Nisenans were moved out of the area in 1855 to reservations in the Sacramento Valley and then later to Round Valley in Mendocino County.

Some were located in nearby camps called "campoodies." But into the twentieth century, miners kept trying to take away even this small remnant of the lands that had been occupied by the Nisenans for centuries.

As early as 1852, the Nevada County census showed that emigrant Chinese already outnumbered the native Indians, 3886 to 3226. By 1870, only nine Indians were listed in the census.

Chief Charlie Cully (right) and Betsy and Josie (above), some of the last of the Nevada County Nisenan Indians.

BOOMS AND BUSTS

A boom followed by a bust was the usual cycle of gold mining towns. What was here today could be gone tomorrow. And that was true of some of the rapidly shifting settlements in Nevada County.

Most of the miners who rushed in during 1849 rushed right back out again to avoid the boredom, isolation, discomfort, and deprivation that came along with harsh winter rains and snows.

But when they rushed back in again as soon as the mud and snow embargo was lifted in early February 1850, they found that Nevada City boasted a lively population of about 2000 with thousands more camping in tents, brush houses, and a few log cabins in a radius of four miles. The town grew so rapidly it was dubbed "Mushroom City." Settlements at Gold Run and Rough and Ready were also mushrooming.

At nearby Coyoteville, miners were burrowing in with a fury. And many were planning to stay throughout the winter.

Mr. Olney was elected Justice of the Peace under the rules of the new California Constitution. He died soon after leaving a verbal will for the "boys" to have a "jolly good time" with the $6000 he left behind. The boys—and the local merchants—did just that.

Flour, pork, and moldy biscuits were selling for from $1 to $5 a pound. Whiskey and brandy went at $6 to $8 a bottle, and molasses for $8 a gallon.

But what did it matter?

In the Gold Run area, "pound diggins" were yielding about 12 troy ounces of gold per day per man. One miner along Gold Run and Deer Creek reportedly sold his 150 foot claim for $10,000 and headed for home. And—he claimed—that wasn't a high price as one-eighth of another claim went for $4000.

Sinking a "coyote" shaft (Courtesy of Darwin Publications).

During the spring and summer of 1850, a more permanent settlement began to form in Nevada City. Streets were laid out, lots—free for the taking—were surveyed, bridges were built, and mining water ditches were being dug. A livery stable and a number of wooden shake merchandise stores nudged each other as they lined up along Main and Commercial Streets. For $25 a week, you could lodge at the new hotel "of sorts," the Nevada Hotel. You could even find relatively current Eastern newspapers in the " reading room" of a new "two-story" building.

The sounds of laughter, fiddling, and singing along with shouts and shots and the clank of shovels and the click of dice filled the air.

Although prices fell as more supplies came in, merchants were jubilant. While the weather was good and the roads were passable, they stashed away a big supply of goods hoping for even higher profits than during the previous winter when rain and snow clogged the routes to the foothills.

Then along came Trouble—with a big T.

When the rains stopped, the creeks dried up, and the miners, who could no longer get water to wash their diggings, packed up their meager belongings and left.

Prices sank and, one by one, merchants closed their doors. The doom and gloom boys predicted Nevada City was a "goner."

But they were wrong—as they were to be over and over again. The citizens of both Nevada City and Grass Valley—again and again—found ways to endure not only rainless summers but mud- and snow-clogged winters along with fires and floods.

When the rains returned in the fall, so did the miners in greater and greater numbers.

By 1851, 250 buildings stood shoulder-to-shoulder in Nevada City, and mining operations and businesses were once again "booming."

MORE THAN GOLD
Felix Gillet

Some of the early settlers who came to the gold country discovered more than gold.

John Studebaker, the automobile manufacturer, got his start in Placerville making wheelbarrows for miners. And you can bet your best pair of "designer" jeans that Levi Strauss got the idea for mass-producing blue jeans when he sold his last bolt of canvas tenting to a gold miner to make a pair of heavy-duty pants. Philip D. Armour first began to carve out a career as a butcher in Placerville before he went on to build a fat fortune in the Eastern packing and slaughtering business. And, at first, Brannan didn't do badly selling his gold pans and other supplies to gold-rushers.

In 1852, Felix Gillet, a young, short, dapper, French ex-sailor wearing a silk stovepipe hat over a head filled with big ideas stepped off a steamer in Boston, Massachusetts for a two-year visit with Mrs. Julia Ward Howe—poet, author, composer of "The Battle Hymn of the Republic," and activist in the anti-slavery and women's suffrage movements. During his stay in Boston, Gillet learned the barber trade.

In 1858, he moved on to California, stopping first in San Jose and then moving on to open a barber shop in Nevada City in February 1859.

In between giving shaves, haircuts, and shampoos, Gillet sold fancy stationery that he had imported from France and studied and planned to realize an old dream.

In 1871, he bought 20 acres on a barren piece of land on Aristocra-

Felix Gillet.

cy Hill on the outskirts of Nevada City. Then he ordered $3000 worth of plants—basically deciduous fruit and nut trees—from a nursery in France.

His friends thought he was a little "nuts," but Gillet ignored their skepticism. In a descriptive mood that was either defiant or humorous, he named his acreage the Barren Hill Nursery and set to work proving the name to be inaccurate. (And that's how Nursery Street later got its name.)

Gillet cleared and cultivated his acreage and hauled in load after load of good top soil—all by hand. Reportedly, he would allow no animal-powered cultivation. And for some unknown reason, instead of taking a lesson from all the water carrying ditches and flumes in the area, he dug a well and carried water to his plants bucket, by bucket, by endless bucket. (Perhaps memories of these early water-carrying days were behind his later vigorous and successful backing of a Nevada City municipal water plant.)

All his hard work paid off, for in a few years his orchard, garden, and nursery were a showplace with hardly a weed daring to intrude.

Gillet also kept meticulous weather records and researched and experimented with chestnuts, filberts, almonds, walnuts, grapes, prunes, raising silkworms—unsuccessfully—and making wine—successfully. In addition to all that, he wrote many articles for horticultural journals and newspapers and carried on long correspondences with people throughout the world.

And there is more.

As his nursery and other vocations and avocations flourished, Gillet imported seeds and plant stock from France and other foreign countries and redistributed them throughout the U.S.

Some say Gillet was the father of the Persian (English) walnut industry in Northern California and Oregon. He is also credited with having been the distributor of the large groves of filberts in the Willamette Valley of Oregon. He also gained fame as a floriculturist.

In his day, Gillet was as well-known as Luther Burbank and was ranked second to Burbank in importance to developments in California agriculture.

Gillet was also a civic-minded man who was actively involved in local politics and issues. He served as town trustee of Nevada City from 1878 to 1880, he was elected to the Advanced Horticultural Board of State Viticulture Commissioners, and was appointed by the county supervisors as a Horticulture Commissioner.

Gillet was also a man of principle who was not afraid to speak his mind or show where he stood—or sat.

At a political rally prior to the Civil War, some local officials were reportedly reluctant to sit on the same platform with a black man who was to be a speaker. Gillet wasn't. He sat next to him.

In contrast, Gillet's tolerance did not extend to all races. Like many in the community at the time, Gillet felt the "Chinese must go."

In April 1880, the California Legislature passed a law to remove all Chinese outside the limits of incorporated towns and cities. The reason usually given for this action was that many devastating fires started in ramshackle Chinatowns.

Soon after, Judge Lake of San Francisco notified the marshal of Nevada City that removal of the Chinese from the city limits was unlawful and legal redress would be sought if Nevada City Chinese were "impressed or molested."

Undaunted, trustee Gillet declared that he would enforce the removal of the Chinese "at all hazards." He was saved the "hazard" when a disastrous fire struck Nevada City on June 5, 1880 and leveled Chinatown behind Broad Street.

After the fire, Gillet sent a note to an attorney representing local Chinese saying, "Do not trouble yourself over Chinatown. It has gone to hell. Removed by fire."

Another type of emigration also plagued Gillet.

In the beginning—like so many beginnings—there were no wormy apples in California. But codling moth worms had appeared first in the valley and then worked their way into the foothills.

In July 1881, Gillet reported to local papers that the codling moths were playing havoc with apples and pears in his orchard, and he was trying to get rid of them by scraping the trees so the exposed pupae could be destroyed. He gave instructions on how he was doing it and urged others to do the same.

Despite Gillet's repeated warnings and instructions, in September 1881, codling worms ruined almost the entire local apple and pear crops.

When the State Board of Horticulture subsequently appointed William Boggs as the Inspector of Fruit Pests, Gillet resigned his position on the board in protest. Apparently, Gillet felt Boggs didn't know beans about bugs. (Gillet may have been right, for the codling moths are still with us today.)

Gillet died in 1908 and was buried in Pioneer Cemetery in Nevada City.

A bronze plaque on the Nevada City hall honors him as one of the pioneer councilmen in the first city hall. One at Nursery Street also honors him for enriching the "horticulture of the world" through his work with "walnuts, filberts, chestnuts, and prunes."

NEVADA CITY'S
GRANDEST PLAN
(and How It Failed)

You know how modern-day politicians are when making grand plans. A billion here and a billion there, and soon it adds up to some real money. Well, things were much the same in 1851, but on a somewhat smaller scale.

On a heady spring day in 1851, several citizens filled with high hopes for the future of the area drew up a scheme for the incorporation of Nevada City on a grandiose scale. Some truly wanted a more orderly community. Others had decided that all the gold wasn't in them "thar" hills, and they wanted to lay claim to a high-ranking prestigious office with a high-paying prestigious salary.

When word was received that the city charter had been approved by the California Legislature, things got off to a quick but awkward start. Before Hamlet Davis, the newly elected mayor, could pound his gavel, he was ousted. The election had been premature as the city charter was not yet official.

At the next election, a Mayor and ten Aldermen were elected. They were the Common Council. The Council then elected a Treasurer, Assessor, Clerk, Attorney, Marshal, and Recorder. Then things rolled into high gear.

First, the Council bought a City Hall. Then they built a jail. Next, they bought a hospital. They all filled rapidly, and expenses went up and up.

Since many taxes went uncollected and only a few license fees found their way into the city coffers, this big city government was soon in big trouble.

A public meeting was held in September 1851 to discuss the problem.

During the meeting, the Aldermen decided their best laid plans had certainly gone "agley" and that they should discharge all city employees and suspend operation. Naturally, the salaried officials objected. But their objections were soon silenced when the people overwhelmingly agreed with the Aldermen.

The city charter was repealed in early 1852 after being in effect for less than a year. The script issued by the city for more than $8000 was never redeemed, but samples of it were valued as a memento of the first and grandest plan that Nevada City officials had ever goofed. (At least that's what the writers of Thompson and West's *History of Nevada County, California* claimed in 1880. Other historians may someday pass this dubious honor on to a later city government.)

But the scheme was not a complete fiasco for everyone. One crafty official quickly discovered a way to make his lucrative job even more lucrative. Recorder Thomas Freeman was actually empowered to act only as a municipal judge. And while he was entitled to settle disputes over mining claims, miners mistakenly thought Freeman could also record mining claims. Freeman never told them differently, and he did a brisk business. As the miners poured through his office, he would ceremoniously go through the dignified and seemingly official motions of carefully recording mining claim after mining claim for which he then collected an outrageously high fee.

By the time the city government folded, Freeman didn't have a worry. He simply retired—wealthy.

THAT'S
ENTERTAINMENT???

The most popular pastime in the early mining camps was checking out what was going on at the local gambling saloons. Every camp of any size had one or more. And at the end of a hard day's work, the miners would leave their diggins in swarms and fly straight to the nearest one—like moths to a flame.

They seldom left until their gambling fever had burned them—badly.

As early as 1851 Nevada City had two "magnificent" saloons, the Empire and Barker's Exchange, which faced each other across Main Street. The miners in the Grass Valley area flocked to the Alta.

At each of these places, "men only" could drink all the "tanglefoot whiskey" they could hold, listen to lively tunes by a band of live musicians (that's the only way they came, then), and try their luck at monte, faro, chuck-a-luck, twenty-one, roulette, and other games on from 12 to 15 different gambling tables in each of these saloons.

Monte was a favorite way miners lessened the weight of their "pokes" of gold.

Stakes were often high and a large crowd would flock around to watch the outcome of the turn of a card. If the card didn't turn up right—and usually it didn't—many a miner would head back to the diggins and write home:

"Dear Wife: No money to send. The pickin's are slim."

Maybe the pickin's were slim for him, but certainly not for the gambling houses, which did a particularly thriving business on Sundays.

Even itinerant preachers would sometimes stop by the saloons on Sunday where they were sure to find the largest crowd. The games would stop for a short time while the minister led the crowd in singing a few hymns. The preacher would then say a few words and take up a collection. The miners were usually generous. As soon as the minister left, the games would go on.

Preaching and gambling weren't the only action in the saloons. Frequently, these early "rushers" practiced how to keep their feet fleet by playing "dodge the bullet."

If a hot argument erupted in a saloon, which they did frequently, weapons—usually a gun or a knife—would be drawn and the onlookers would rush for the nearest exit. Within a few minutes the argument would be settled, sometimes permanently, and the crowd would surge back into the saloon as the dealers monotonously intoned, "Place your bets, Gentlemen. Place your bets."

Other forms of entertainment that were less brutal to the miner's "poke" but more brutal to the contestants were dog fights, chicken fights, prizefights, and bear and bull battles.

Although these fights were supposedly opposed by the "better portion" of the community, they drew large crowds. Bear and bull fights were especially popular.

In these fights, a bear, usually lazy or half tame, would be chained to a post so he wouldn't run away in fright or decide to attack the crowd in revenge. Then a bull would be run into the arena and prodded into attacking the often reluctant bear.

Even a few of the "better portions" of the community sometimes got caught up in the heat of the battle. Or so a popular story goes.

One bear was just about to have his day when he got loose in the arena, chased out his human tormentors, and charged toward the crowd. As he tried to lumber over the arena fence, the crowd jumped from their seats and rushed for the hinterland—except for two.

Every time the bear would put his paws on the fence rail, heavy-bearded (this is important) Dr. Kendall and C. F. Wood would beat the bear's paws back with a shovel and a heavy cane. The battle was a stalemate until the bear gave himself a mighty heave up and came face to face with hairy-faced (this is still important) Dr. Kendall. For a second, the bear gazed into Kendall's eyes, then muttered, "Et tu, Brute?" and fell over dead from a broken heart.

Another early form of entertainment was telling tall tales.

Large crowds were also attracted to jury trials—legal and illegal—and execution of sentences—legal and illegal—that included shaving beards and heads, brandings, whippings, and hangings.

Some miners took delight in going out and "exterminating" a few

Caroline Chapman.

Lola Montez.

Indians or at least shooting up their rancherias to get in a little target practice. Apparently some also thought it was fun to start fires—many of the early fires were incendiary—and watch others spend a lot of time trying to put them out.

Many of the miners spent their Sundays by "laying in provisions" and doing other menial chores such as cooking, washing their alternate pair of trousers, and writing letters home. A few attended church services held on the streets or under trees or in any available cabin or shanty by a minister of any denomination.

Other forms of entertainment were billiards and bowling and watching the tri-weekly stages come and go. Miners could also enjoy smoking a good cigar while reading relatively recent newspapers in the reading room in Nevada City. By April 1851 they could read all the latest local news in the *Nevada Journal.*

By 1865, they could watch horse races at Glenbrook Park, which was touted as one of the finest race courses on the Pacific Coast.

On just about any day of the week, they could watch impromptu fist fights, pistol duels, and name-calling contests. And, yes, before many years had passed, they could visit one of a number of brothels or smoke a little opium at a local den.

The more sophisticated form of popular entertainment was

attending the theaters. By 1852, Grass Valley, Rough and Ready, and Nevada City all had theaters. Some of the best performers of the time, including The Robinson Family, the Chapman Family, Edwin Booth, Kate Hayes, Horace Greeley, Mark Twain, Lola Montez, Emma Nevada, and James Marshall, came to act, sing, dance, or lecture in these theaters. They were usually greeted with polite attention or roaring applause and showers of gold coins. But not always.

When Hugh F. McDermott appeared as Shakespeare's *Richard III* in December 1856, his fame had spread to Nevada City before him. Local theatergoers turned out in mass to show they could give him the same type of reception he had previously received in San Francisco, Sacramento, and Marysville.

When McDermott appeared on the stage as the misshapen Richard and went into his histrionic antics he was immediately greeted with a deluge of cabbages, potatoes, eggs, flour, pepper, tripe, sausages, and pumpkins—all watered down by squirt guns. The barrage was accompanied by catcalls and uncomplimentary bits of artistic criticism.

When Richard handed his sword to Queen Anne and she asked, "What shall I say or do?" a hundred impatient miners yearning for a real tragedy shouted, "Kill him! Kill him!"

This abuse was repeated every time McDermott appeared in a scene. Although he begged for mercy, he received none. McDermott refused to die and be buried under a sea of moldy produce. Instead he stalked off the stage like a king, leaving the cabbages behind him. And so the curtain closed on one of McDermott's many painful performances.

JENNY LIND
BOWS OUT

Theaters, like the traveling troupes that performed in them in the gold rush days, had a way of coming and going rapidly. Most of them went up in flames. But Nevada City's Jenny, after a brief stay, bowed out in a more ladylike manner.

Although Jenny Lind, the singing Swedish Nightingale, never sang in California, her successful tour of Eastern cities in 1850 and 1852 caught the fancy of name-dropping Californians. They named everything from clipper ships and gambling houses to mining camps and theaters after her.

The Jenny Lind Theatre built and rebuilt by Jim McGuire after it burned twice in the early 1850s was the most magnificent theater in San Francisco. A less pretentious Jenny Lind Theatre was built during the summer of 1850 at the foot of Main Street in Nevada City. Since Deer Creek was calm and peaceful at the time, Jenny was built to jut out over the scenic creek with some of her supporting props resting in the water.

The theater was opened with the Chapman family on November 20, 1851. At every performance, Jenny echoed with the wild cannonading applause given to the young ladies in the cast by the young male theatergoers, who were starved for a rare glimpse of the feminine species—of any age.

Then in early March 1852, a severe wind, snow, and rain storm raged for several days. Rivers and creeks cascaded in torrents down the steep mountain canyons. Once peaceful Deer Creek "boomed" as drift wood banged against anything in its path.

Jenny Lind.

On one of these dark and stormy nights, Jenny got into trouble, and everyone expected her to leave town soon.

When a log smashed one of Jenny's support pillars, a group worked hastily to carry the scenery out of Jenny and store it in a higher and safer place.

Early the next morning, a crowd began to gather to watch the action.

A shrieking woman trapped in her house by the rapidly rising water was rescued by a miner who waded across the roaring stream and carried her to safety on his back.

The crowd grew larger as they waited expectantly to see bridges and houses wash away.

Shortly after noon, a heavy log shoved the Main Street bridge off its foundation, and the debris rushed downstream toward Jenny.

The crowd began to shout and run for a closer look.

A few blocks away a court battle raged over who owed what to whom for the recently constructed Jenny. At the sound of the

Nevada City in 1852 after the flood (Courtesy California State Library).

commotion outside, everyone in the courthouse rushed out to see what was going on.

As a huge log smashed into Jenny and knocked out her remaining props, Jenny bowed slightly and amid shouts of "There she goes!" slipped into the stream and floated gracefully on the billowing foam before smashing into the Illinois Boarding House that also joined the procession.

When Jenny first bowed into the water, Lawyer Lorenzo Sawyer said, "That's a lien that will take priority over all our claims." (You'll read more about Sawyer and water later.)

Within a short time, Jenny was a complete wreck and soon after everyone lost interest in the law suit.

Some say that Jenny went down the stream with her American flag waving proudly behind her. Another report says that Jenny was an almost total shambles as soon as she hit the water. Whichever way she went, she departed with much more grace than Hugh F. McDermott. And other theaters soon rose to take her place.

Jenny's departure did the town one last great service. When another disastrous fire broke out in September 1852, the entire city would have been destroyed except the fire couldn't leap the gap left by Jenny and the building she knocked out on her way out of town.

DON'T FORGET THE LADIES—
Lola, Lotta, and Emma Nevada

Lola

In July 1853, Lola Montez and her newest husband, Patrick Hull, rode into Grass Valley on the stage from Marysville. Their arrival created a hubbub that some said would have "awakened the dead." Poor Patrick didn't last long as Lola's husband or as a popular historical figure. But people in the area still talk about Lola's visit as if it were only yesterday, and her restored home on Mill Street is a historical site that most tourists still seek out.

What was it that made Lola so popular then and now?

Lola was young, she was beautiful (to most), she was interesting, and she had a way of getting attention. She also had an untamable spirit that many found irresistible. She once reportedly said, "I want to live before I die." And she did—on a grand worldwide scale.

Before her arrival, her reputation as the divine, eccentric, wild, wanton, fabulous, flamboyant, tempestuous, and—this above all— "scandalous" Lola Montez had spread even to remote, rustic Grass Valley. Miners had already named a placer mine the Lola Montez Diggins on Lola Montez Hill.

What were the events and incidents that had won Lola such notoriety?

To begin at the beginning and name just a few, Lola was born Marie Dolores—the diminutive of which is Lola—Eliza Rosanna Gilbert in Limerick, Ireland on July 3, 1818. (In her biography, Lola

Lola Montez.

gives her birth date as 1824, which has led to much historical confusion as to Lola's age at various times and places.)

Since her father was an Army Captain, the family was soon transferred to India. About three years later, her father died and Dolores was sent to England to be educated.

In 1837, rather than marry an elderly judge—"a gouty old rascal"—to whom she had been betrothed by her mother, Dolores at the age of 19 eloped with young Captain (or Lieutenant) Thomas James taking her beautiful trousseau with her.

Soon after, the couple returned to India where Captain James and a "friend," Mrs. Lomer, went out for one of their frequent social horseback rides and never returned.

Dolores cried a little, laughed a little, and decided to become a famous dancer.

After studying in Madrid, she returned to London as the mysterious Spanish dancer, Lola Montez.

Lola gained some limited success in London performing her

somewhat shocking "La Tarantella," the Spider Dance. Then she moved on to perform in Paris, Brussels, Berlin, Dresden, Bonn, St. Petersburg, and Warsaw.

During her tour, Lola collected an impressive list of admirers, lovers, and friends including Franz Liszt, the famous pianist, and Alexandre Dumas, Victor Hugo, and Honore de Balzac, famous authors. She also captivated an ill-fated fiance, Monsieur Dujarrier, a journalist, who was killed in a pistol duel that he didn't have a chance of winning because he couldn't hit the "broad side of a barn" and his opponent was one of the best shots in Paris.

One of Lola's biggest claims to fame and notoriety came in Munich where King Ludwig I of Bavaria was so fascinated by Lola's "charms" that he built her a villa, gave her funds, and promoted her to the rank of Countess of Landsfeld. However, when the Countess helped start a revolution by dabbling in politics and freely expressing and promoting her liberal views, the King was forced to order Lola's arrest. Lola escaped "in the nick of time" and returned to London.

There she married George Heald and had to flee England to avoid being arrested for bigamy. Lola had failed to get a divorce from the long-gone Captain James.

Again Lola had escaped imprisonment and left behind yet another husband. She then brought her act to the U.S. in 1851.

During her tour of Eastern cities, Lola received mixed reviews: some praised her dancing, others criticized it.

In May 1853, she arrived in San Francisco where talented theatrical people usually played to packed houses. That wasn't always so with Lola.

Since everyone was eager to see the notorious Lola, her first-night performances were usually sellouts. However, seeing Lola perform once must have been enough. After a few appearances in an area, attendance would fall and Lola would take her act back "on the road."

One critic said that as a "danseuse" Lola was strictly " mechanical" and "without grace," and her beauty was "nothing to boast of" except her eyes and mouth were "fascinating."

Sometimes a few in her audiences were foolhardy enough to boo and hiss. They should have known better for Lola didn't take criticism lightly. Usually she retaliated by nailing an antagonist with her flashing dark eyes and giving him a flaming tongue lashing. She was also not hesitant at times to grab her riding crop or anything she could lay her hands on and attempt to give a critic a sound beating.

In San Francisco, Lola played the leading role in *Lola Montez in Bavaria,* a play that she claimed she had written about incidents of her life in Bavaria.

Some critics who liked Lola's dancing found her acting "boring." A burlesque of Lola's play called *Who's Got the Countess?* starred Caroline Chapman who performed the "Spy-Dear" dance. That play soon outdrew Lola's play and made Lola such a laughingstock that she left San Francisco and headed for Sacramento and Marysville.

Before she left, Lola answered the play's question when Patrick Hull, a journalist, married the Countess in San Francisco in early July 1853.

Lola's performances in Sacramento and Marysville were first greeted with enthusiasm followed by nearly empty houses and ridicule answered by flaming outbursts from the "flaming beauty."

More trouble came in Marysville when the newlyweds quarreled and either Lola threw Patrick out of their hotel room or Patrick left to get some peace and quiet.

Still, the couple did arrive together in Grass Valley in July 1853. And much of Lola's fascinating story had traveled to the area ahead of her.

Again the pattern repeated. Lola's arrival created a sensation and she played at double the usual prices to jam-packed houses during her first performances at the Alta Theatre in Grass Valley and at Dramatic Hall in Nevada City. The applause was said to have even drowned out the eternal 24-hour clatter of the local stamp mills. Then attendance fell off. At her last scheduled performance in Grass Valley, the audience was so small Lola returned their money and refused to perform.

Some writers claim that having acquired a "distaste" for men and the world Lola had come to Grass Valley to seek seclusion and peace. This seems unlikely because at the time Grass Valley was by no means just another tiny mining camp. Rustic, it was; but it was also the sixth largest town in California. Nevada City was even bigger.

Lola had obviously come to the area to perform. Then when attendance quickly fell off, she probably decided that touring the smaller and more remote mining camps would not be profitable so she settled down for a time.

She apparently didn't seek peace and quiet either. Not unless you call it restful to orchestrate weekly and semiweekly "salons" in a grand Parisian style for the local "gentry" and mine owners along with visiting musicians, performers, investors, and businessmen. This Lola did with the financial support of John Southwick, part owner of the Empire mine, just as soon as she settled into the cottage on Mill Street, which she later bought when Gilmor Meredith, the owner, returned East.

During these well-attended parties, Lola served excellent brandy, passed around "passable" cigars, demonstrated her player piano, talked about her life in Bavaria and abroad, sang foreign songs in several languages, and, in general, captivated her audience by proving that when she wanted to she could be "very agreeable."

At times, Lola would don her stage costume and give private performances of her famous Spider Dance. Commenting on these parties, which he attended, Meredith said Lola couldn't "dance a common pas set."

In also describing Lola and one of her parties to which he wasn't invited, Edwin F. Morse, who lived near Lola's cottage, commented many years later that Lola's "charms" were beginning to fade and she was usually "frankly disgusting" and slatternly and often looked like she needed a good washing. (Of course, this might have been a big case of sour grapes delivered by a socially snubbed neighbor.)

Some claim that Lola's extravagant parties financially ruined Southwick. Others contend that her parties helped develop the Empire mine by convincing capitalists to invest in it.

In October 1853, a local paper reported that Lola had apparently decided she was tired of "Hully wedlock" and had applied for a divorce. Hull left town.

As Lola discarded Hull, she gathered around her not only a bevy of admirers but a menagerie of animals that included: canaries, dogs, sheep, a goat, horse, wild cat, parrot, lamb, and a grizzly bear that she kept chained to a tree. That is until the grizzly had the temerity to bite Lola's hand while she was feeding it. Lola sold the bear, which was probably used in a bear and dog fight at nearby Storms' Ranch.

Lola's stay in Grass Valley evoked many stories, some of which may or may not be true.

Some say she was a generous and kindly person who would spend hours caring for sick miners. Others pointed out that she only tended to "single" miners, which many of them were at the time.

Lola probably taught little Lotta Crabtree a few dance steps, and she may have encouraged Lotta to get on the blacksmith's anvil in

Fippin blacksmith shop in Rough and Ready.

Rough and Ready to perform. However, some historians question whether Lola tried to get Lotta to go on tour with her.

But some of the tales do have some basis in fact as reported in local memoirs and newspapers.

Although Lola may have been shunned by some of the ladies, she apparently was kind to children. And she did throw a nice party for a group of small girls during the Christmas season of 1853. The group "may" have included little Lotta Crabtree.

In January 1854, Lola "flashed like a meteor" through the snow-flakes and "wanton snowballs" as she toured Nevada City in a sleigh pulled by a span of horses decorated with impromptu cow bells.

Lola narrowly escaped death or serious injury in May 1854. While she was trying to jump her horse across a ditch to pick some wild flowers, the horse stumbled on the steep bank, tossed Lola, and barely missed landing on top of her.

Lola took a pack trip to Truckee Meadows in July 1854 along with a group that included Alonzo Delano, well-known humorist, writer, banker, miner, trader, speculator, and Wells, Fargo agent. On the return trip, one of the men in the party got lost and was missing for a few days, but eventually turned up hungry, tired, and footsore but safe.

Alonzo—the humorist—reported he enjoyed the trip "hugely notwithstanding the eccentricities of 'the divine Lola'." It was hinted that the trip broke up early because some of the campers couldn't stand Lola's "eccentricities."

On this trip, Lola may or may not have suggested the name for Independence Lake in honor of the Fourth of July Independence Day.

Lola once complained that newspapers had given her the honor of horse whipping hundreds of men she had never seen. However, in November 1854, Lola did try to horsewhip Henry Shipley, editor of the *Grass Valley Telegraph*, for reprinting some unkind remarks made in a New York paper about Lola and her European friends.

On reading Shipley's report, Lola bolted out of her cottage with the offending paper in one hand and her riding whip in the other and charged down the street to the Golden Gate Saloon (now the Holbrooke Hotel) where Shipley, an alcoholic, could usually be found. A curious crowd followed in Lola's stormy wake.

Lola blazed into the saloon and attempted to whip Shipley about the head, but Shipley caught her by the arm and took her whip away. Lola then fired off her tongue and demanded an apology. Shipley only stepped back and coolly smoked his pipe. (Editors in those days were often faced with more dire dangers than a lady's whip and tongue. Several were soundly beaten with a cane or shot and killed.)

Lola appealed to the "honest miners" for their aid. The miners simply laughed. Lola then asked them to have a free drink on her. When they refused—a most uncharacteristic response—Lola left the field of battle in defeat.

Lola later wrote that she was forced to use her riding whip, which had never been used on the back of a horse, to whip an "Ass."

Some writers suggest that Shipley was so shamed by the incident that he left the area and committed suicide. This seems unlikely. Shipley was clearly the victor in the fracas; and although he did leave Grass Valley soon after, he only went as far as Nevada City to become the editor of the *Nevada Democrat*. His subsequent suicide was probably triggered by ill health and alcoholism and not the run-in with Lola. However, Lola apparently did go into seclusion for a time after the incident.

Lola then left Grass Valley in May 1855 never to return.

In June 1855 she left to tour Australia where she met with little success—except in evoking more scandals—before she returned to San Francisco.

By October 1856, a San Francisco paper stated that it was plain that Lola's "dancing days" were over, and they were. Soon after, Lola sold her cottage in Grass Valley, retired from the stage, and returned to New York where she made a living giving how-to-keep-your-beauty lectures. Grace Greenwood, a leading female correspondent, reported that she found Lola's lectures even "more demoralizing than her dancing."

Lola died in New York at the age of 42 on January 17, 1861. On her gravestone in the Greenwood Cemetery in Brooklyn is the simple epitaph: Mrs. Eliza Gilbert.

Lotta

When Mrs. Mary Crabtree came to Grass Valley in 1853, she brought with her something just as precious and just as much in demand as gold—six-year-old, pretty, round-faced, red-haired, black-eyed, vivacious Lotta.

Mary Ann Livesey had married the handsome but shiftless John Crabtree in New York, and almost immediately discovered her mistake. While she worked at her trade as an upholsterer, John squandered their income by trying to run a small bookstore while dreaming up get-rich-quick schemes.

Lotta was born to the couple in 1847. From the beginning, Mary focused all her love, time, energy, talent, and ambition on the bubbling child.

While listening to all the stories about riches to be found in California for the pickin', John caught a late case of gold fever and headed for San Francisco in 1852. In the spring of 1853, Mary and Lotta followed only to find that John had wandered into the high Sierra.

Eventually John sent word for Mary to join him in Grass Valley where he had plans for a great adventure. When Mary and Lotta arrived in 1853, they discovered John's grand plan. Reluctantly, Mary joined in the venture, and they opened a less-than-first-class, two-story boarding house on Mill Street in Grass Valley.

Mary had her dreams, too, and they swirled around the theater. In her spare time in both New York and San Francisco, she had taken Lotta with her to the theaters, and she was always alert to the rapidly changing theatrical trends.

Along with the first gold-rushers, theatrical people of all types and

Mrs. Mary Ann Crabtree.

Lotta Crabtree.

nationalities and degrees of talent poured into San Francisco and spread out into the mining camps.

While in Grass Valley, Mary paid close attention as many of the most famous theatrical people of the time passed through. She watched what they did and listened to what they had to say about who was on the way up and who was on the way down and why.

Perhaps that is why the rather straightlaced Mary allowed Lotta to spend time with the less-than-proper but always "stage-center" Lola Montez when she blazed into Grass Valley in 1853 like a comet trailing her flamboyant past behind her. Once again Lola did the unexpected, she bought a cottage just a few doors from the Crabtree's hotel and for a short time enjoyed the rustic life of the mining frontier.

Lola was fond of children and seemingly took a particular fancy to the energetic, irrepressible Lotta to whom she taught some of her dance steps. The naturally talented Lotta quickly mastered the fandango, highland fling, and a few ballet steps with ease.

Just as cows apparently acted as lodestars and guided many a foolish miner to hunks of gold, blacksmiths and their anvils seemed to serve as lodestones that attracted children destined for theatrical fame and fortune.

As the popular story goes, it was Lola who hoisted little Lotta onto the blacksmith's anvil in Rough and Ready and clapped and encouraged Lotta into giving one of her first public performances, which was greeted with wild applause.

In these early days, women and children were still a rarity and easily gained the center of attention anywhere they went in California. And women—such as Caroline Chapman, Lola Montez, Laura Keene, and Kate Hayes—along with children—such as the Bateman children and little Sue Robinson—dominated California theaters. Wherever they appeared, whether in San Francisco or remote mining areas, miners crowded around to see them, and their performances were often greeted with thunderous applause followed by showers of gold and coins.

By the summer of 1854, Lotta's brother, John Ashworth, was born, and father John was ready to continue his search for gold in the remote but booming gold mining area of Rabbit Creek in Sierra County.

Again, John found no gold. Again, Mary ran a boarding house. Again, the fabulous Lola reportedly appeared on the scene. She pleaded with Mary to let her take Lotta on her tour of Australia. Mary, perhaps subconsciously aware of what a real treasure she had in Lotta, refused Lola's offer.

But Lotta was not long without an instructor. Under the tutelage of Mart Taylor, a young Italian, musician, dancer, versifier, cobbler, saloon keeper, theater operator, and dancing school master, Lotta quickly added Irish jigs and reels to her repertoire of dance steps.

Mary put her talented needle to work and whipped up a leprechaun outfit, and Lotta, like a mischievously laughing bundle of magical energy, jigged and reeled her way through a performance that outdrew the more seasoned Sue Robinson. Thunderous applause was followed by showers of coins—naturally.

Not John, but Mary had discovered a real lode of gold.

After Mary scooped up the coins in her calico apron, she and Taylor quickly assembled a company of musicians and off they went to seek further treasures leaving behind a note, fresh baked bread, and a pot of beans for the once-again-absent John.

Away they went traveling from mining camp to mining camp. Black-haired, dark-eyed, tall, graceful Taylor would enter the camp first beating a huge drum and close behind came pretty little Lotta perched on the back of a mule. The combination was a sure winner.

On and on they traveled, higher and higher into the mountains moving like miners from claim to claim into regions where children and women were rarer and rarer and only a few theatrical troupes had climbed before. They played in barrooms and on counters in stores surrounded by sacks of flour and piles of supplies.

Everywhere they were greeted by thunderous applause followed by showers of coins and nuggets. Again and again, Mary untied her apron and scooped up the proceeds from their hard labor.

It was a hard life, but it was a living.

Their travels were interrupted only long enough for Mary to bear another son. Then the little troupe was off again.

At times, Lotta and Mary would venture into San Francisco where they would play day-to-day engagements in sleazy little bar-theaters along the waterfront.

Once again the irrepressible Lola caught up with them in San Francisco. This time she begged to take Lotta to Paris. Again, Mary refused.

And so the pattern repeated itself time and time again, year after year. Lotta would occasionally get a choice part in one of the better theaters of San Francisco only to be replaced by the better managed Sue Robinson. Then the little troupe would regroup and make wider and longer circuits of mining camps in the mountains and in the valleys.

As competition from other troupes got tougher in the more settled valley camps, Lotta added more and more to her repertoire. Mary made the costumes, applied the makeup, played the triangle, appeared in bit parts, and fiercely guarded her golden treasure by putting up a fire barrier of motherly protection that prevented Lotta from having any intimate contacts or lasting friendships. Yet, the mutual devotion of the two was unmistakable.

In time, Lotta was well-known and acclaimed throughout the mountains and up and down the valleys, but she was still relatively unknown in the better theaters in San Francisco.

Then when variety shows became the popular form of theater in San Francisco in 1859, Lotta's success was assured. For Lotta's talent was nothing if not varied.

She was a mixture of diversity in character and repertoire. She was sturdy and delicate, rowdy and aloof. She did Irish jigs and reels, highland flings, polkas, hornpipes, and softshoe. She was Topsy, a wild Irish boy, a Cockney, and an American sailor. In blackface she strummed the banjo and did " breakdowns." For contrast, she donned white cambric dresses and sang a few sentimental songs.

Suddenly she was in great demand at many of the popular small theaters that sprang up in San Francisco. She was known as " La Petite Lotta, the Celebrated Danseuse and Vocalist," "Miss Lotta, the Unapproachable," and "Miss Lotta, the San Francisco Favorite."

She was a "star."

Following the Washoe strike in 1859, Lotta and her troupe widened their circuit and traveled through the mining camps in the Comstock Lode and on to Portland, Oregon, and back to San Francisco.

As she neared the age of 16, Lotta played more risque parts, showing her ankles and "a little more" as she romped and frolicked through hoydenish parts.

And, yet, strict Mary continued to maneuver the difficult trick of keeping Lotta isolated while in the midst of adoring crowds. Lotta never mingled with fellow actors and seemed not to be a "theater person" at all. To most, she truly was "Miss Lotta, the Unapproachable."

On and on Lotta went, round and round in wider and wider circles like a whirling dervish rising higher and higher on the pinnacle of popularity and fame while amassing more and more rewards. From California she traveled East in 1864 where she took first New York and then the East by storm. Then on to capture the Middle West and round to the South.

At long last she was realizing her mother's lifelong dream, she was winning wide acclaim by appearing in "legitimate" theaters in plays that were written for her. One of her most popular plays was an adaptation of Dickens' *The Old Curiosity Shop* in which Lotta played both Little Nell and the Marchioness. In *The Little Detective* she impersonated six characters.

Round and round the theater circuits she went, adding more and more plays to her repertoire and more and more boisterous "bits of business"—such as hiking her skirts a little higher, playing more masculine roles, which was still considered daring at the time, and smoking.

Then back she dashed briefly to California in August 1869 to receive more wild acclaim in San Francisco where theaters had become "more civilized" and private boxes were now filled with rich displays of jewels and lavish dresses.

Along with many gold watches, a golden wreath for her hair set with diamonds and a pile of golden "eagles" were added to her treasure trove.

Up and up the ladder of success she scampered bubbling with laughter.

Then came a short hiatus. In 1873, the entire family went "abroad" for about a year. For a time, Lotta played the proper lady and studied French, piano, and painting in Paris. Then she moved to Cheshire, England where the family was reunited, including the often-missing John. Lotta continued the role of a young lady in a light novel of the time. She dressed in white muslin and blue ribbons and drove in a pony cart, but did no acting. Lotta was nearly 27 at the time but looked 18.

Then back she went into the same whirlwind of performances and travel, which extended to England. During this time, she donated her famous Lotta Fountain to take care of thirsty horses in San Francisco.

In New Orleans the Grand Duke Alexis presented her with a set of bracelets and a necklace set with diamonds and turquoise and gave

Lotta Crabtree.

a dinner in her honor on a Russian warship. Each officer was allowed to sit by her side for only ten minutes.

It has been reported that after some performances Lotta would drive her carriage furiously for hours to work off tension. And at times, she could be seen curled up in a railroad coach alone and smoking furiously. But despite these glimpses of a less-than-happy person off the stage, on-stage Lotta always caught fire and burned with a happy fury that critics could never describe. They would usually fall back on the stock phrase that she was "like no one in the world."

In 1891 at the age of 45, Lotta retired. She said she had decided to retire while she was still popular.

Lotta was not only still popular, she was rich. During all their years of travel, Mary had wisely invested in real estate and had amassed a fortune.

Lotta built a spacious lakeside home in the hills of New Jersey and the family—mother, father, and two brothers—gathered around her for a time. John once again retreated to England where he died. In time, the two brothers and Mary died.

Lotta retained her youthful looks for years. At the age of 50, she could have passed for 25 or 30. In contrast, her mother aged more rapidly than most. At the time of her death in 1905, she could have been mistaken for Lotta's great grandmother. But their bond of common devotion was enduring and solid to the end.

Although Lotta was now alone and had no close friends, she never tired of throwing impromptu parties where she would dress in her old costumes and act out favorite roles before her guests.

Lotta died in 1924.

Lotta, who had accumulated her wealth from strangers, gave it back to strangers—about $4 million. Many gold-seeking pseudo-heirs came forth to contest Lotta's will, but, like many gold-seekers before them, they failed.

Lotta's will was as diversified as her talents. Her fortune went to help needy veterans of the "Great War," sick people in hospitals, prisoners on their release, needy actors, students of music and agriculture, children of needy families at Christmas, and to care for worn-out horses and stray dogs and to promote laws against vivisection.

Lotta may indeed have been lonely at times, but if she enjoyed performing as much as she appeared to, she not only had many hours but many years of intense joy. She also gave great joy to millions.

Emma Nevada's birthplace in Alpha Diggins (Courtesy of Margaret Trivelpiece).

Emma Nevada

Let's face the music. Even though Lola Montez is probably the best remembered female historical figure to have passed through Nevada County, she really wasn't much of a dancer, singer, or actress. Lotta Crabtree was much more talented and, eventually, much more wealthy.

But do you know who was the greatest soprano singing talent of them all?

She was born in the Alpha diggins in February 1859 to a country doctor, Dr. W. W. Wixom, and his wife, Maria or Kate, who according to "old timers" had once dealt Faro and been a "lookout" at various gambling houses in the local diggins but was nevertheless a "maid of principle."

Alpha was never really much of a "diggins." During its heyday in 1854 and 1855, only 59 votes were cast in an election. By 1861 Alpha was almost unpopulated. That is probably about the time that the Wixoms moved to Nevada City for a short time.

During that period, "little Wixy," who was still a "wee babe" of about three, made her debut standing on a table in the old Baptist Church in Nevada City wrapped in an American flag and singing the "Star Spangled Banner." Her debut was greeted with enthusiastic applause but no shower of gold coins.

Around 1864, the Wixoms moved on to Austin, Nevada when miners were still rushing to the bustling Comstock Lode.

According to a popular story, at an early age Emma would wrap herself in her mother's apron and, like a grand diva draped in silk, sing to the picture of a king and queen on a cigar box.

While in Austin, Emma's singing talent was recognized by Ira Adams, a music teacher, who gave her and other members of the Methodist Church musical training and staged local concerts at which Emma was soon a "star."

Reportedly, Mr. Adams often told "little Wixy" that someday she would sing before real kings and queens.

As with Lotta Crabtree, a blacksmith figured in another popular story about Emma. Bill Alexander, the local Austin blacksmith, claimed that little Emma would sing so beautifully to the rhythm of his beating anvil that it would bring tears to his eyes. And to keep her singing, he would just keep on beating away.

After her mother died in 1873, Emma was sent to Mills Seminary in Oakland for further musical training. Again, her extraordinary talent was recognized and nurtured.

During school vacations, Emma would practice and develop her voice by imitating bird calls and singing to the mountains and the vast, stark high desert.

She also gave two memorable performances.

At the International Hall in Austin when she was 17, Emma sang "You'll Remember Me." A local critic raved that it was "by far the best concert we have ever listened to in Austin, and one which will be long remembered." And it was for a long time.

The next year Emma sang at a benefit that raised about $400 for a "cork leg" for a miner whose leg had been blown off. During this concert she reportedly first sang "Listen to the Mocking Bird," which she eventually made an international hit. She also sang "Home Sweet Home," which, according to popular reports, never failed to leave the audience teary eyed.

In August 1877, Emma set sail with a group of about 100 other young talented students under the tutelage of Dr. Adrian Ebell. They were to travel throughout Europe to study art, literature, music, and drama. Emma and Dr. Wixom agreed that this would be a great opportunity for Emma to meet and sing for the renowned vocal teacher, Madame Marchesi, in Vienna.

The sudden, tragic death of Dr. Ebell while at sea did not stop the spunky young Emma. She went on to keep her appointment with

Madame Marchesi, and, once again, Emma's talent was quickly recognized.

After receiving the news of Ebell's death, Dr. Wixom sailed for Europe to help Emma. When he arrived, he found her happily taking lessons from Marchesi, who highly praised Emma's natural talent and convinced Dr. Wixom to let Emma stay for three years of intensive study and practice.

Then in May 1880, at the age of 21, Emma made her operatic debut at Her Majesty's Opera in London in the role of Amina in Bellini's *La Sonnambula.* For her debut, she chose the stage name of Emma Nevada to pay tribute to both the county where she was born and the state where she grew up.

Although most local historians claim that Emma received immediate acclaim, a local paper reported that some critics thought Emma had appeared on the operatic stage prematurely. She was a "mere girl in looks," and although her voice had "good qualities," it didn't yet have much power and she had "much to learn as an actress." The paper also reported that Emma was a "disappointment" to her Nevada friends who had expected her "to take London by storm."

Emma and Dr. Wixom didn't let this kind of criticism stop them.

According to one historian, the wily Dr. Wixom ensured full houses at some of Emma's early performances by buying big blocks of tickets and passing them out to members of musical societies and musical students at leading London colleges.

Whether her London debut was a success or not, within the next few years, true to Adams' prediction, Emma was receiving requests to sing before most of the crowned heads of Europe and in all the leading capitals and cities of Europe.

Some historians surmise that she sang in more countries and places than any other prima donna except Adelina Patti.

In an interview, Emma once said that about the only important place she hadn't sung was Turkey and that was only because she didn't have time to do everything.

Emma sang most of the world-famous operas in nine different languages, and her coloratura soprano was particularly acclaimed in parts evoking pathos.

In 1881, the famous composer Verdi persuaded Emma to come to Milan where she gave a series of more than 20 performances of *Aida* to packed houses that some say saved the famous La Scala opera house.

Emma Nevada.

Emma also made several successful tours of America to both big cities and little towns where her encores of "Listen to the Mocking Bird" and "Home Sweet Home" never failed to bring wild applause and bittersweet tears.

On one of her American tours, she appeared with the famous contemporary coloratura Adeline Patti. But all was not smooth singing between the two divas.

According to mixed tales, either Emma or Patti once discovered that one of their names (some say it was Emma's, others say it was Patti's) was billed in larger print than the other. Like true prima donnas, either one or the other declared that the show would not go on until workmen climbed up and wiped out part of the lettering to make the names of equal height.

At the height of her career, Emma fell in love with her English manager, Dr. Raymond Palmer. When they married in Paris in October 1885, it was *the* great international social event of the year.

Their daughter, Mignon, named after one of Emma's favorite operatic roles, was born in Paris in 1887.

Emma Nevada.

Throughout her career, the people in the little town of Austin didn't forget Emma, and Emma didn't forget them. In response to the flowers they sent upon her debut at the Theatre Comique in Paris in 1883, Emma sent back a number of photographs of her in various stage costumes and poses.

Although Emma was never showered with nuggets and gold coins (that's just not proper behavior at an opera), she was given expensive gifts by royalty, musicians, composers, and her grateful audiences.

At the Grand Opera House in San Francisco in March 1885, Emma was greeted with "enthusiasm bordering on lunacy" and given a miner's wheelbarrow lined with quartz and filled with white flowers, a gold basin, and silver bricks.

During her 30-year career, the tiny hazel-eyed, auburn-haired Emma also collected an impressive array of descriptive titles starting with "Little Wixy" and "Little Queen of Alpha Diggins" through the "Blue Bird of Austin," "Sage of the Sierra," "Sagebrush Linnet," and "Comstock Nightingale" to the "International Songbird" and ending with the "Nightingale of Paradise."

But neither the expensive presents or the lavish names seemed to affect Emma, and she never forgot the people "back home."

When she returned to Austin during an American tour in December 1885, the horses were unhitched and her carriage was pulled into town by eager male admirers. Her concert was hailed as "two hours of solid luxury."

At the end of the concert she invited her "old friends" to meet her at a reception at the Methodist Episcopal Church where she had sung at the age of seven during its dedication.

After the world-famous diva changed out of her elaborate concert costume, she sat down at the reception and said, "Now, I'm plain Emma Wixom." She also gave part of the proceeds from her concert to pay off the church debt.

At a concert in Vallejo, Emma learned that Ira Adams, her first music instructor, was in the audience. Emma reportedly sang her heart out and bowed to him several times from the stage. Ironically, Adams could not hear her silvery flute-like notes as she sang some of the songs he had first taught her nor the thunderous applause that followed each number. He was now deaf.

When Emma, during her last American tour in 1902, came to sing in the Nevada Theatre to pay tribute to the county where she was born, she was given one of the most royal receptions in the history of the county.

As the band struck up "Auld Lang Syne" when Emma stepped off the Nevada County Narrow Gauge Railroad in Grass Valley, thousands cheered and waved handkerchiefs at the graciously bowing Emma. More thousands lined the streets to applaud as she passed by smiling and waving from her open carriage.

The Laurel Parlor of the Native Daughters had turned Emma's room at the National Hotel into a bower of flowers.

Emma stepped onto the balcony of the National Hotel to bow and wave to the wildly cheering mob below on Broad Street.

The night of her performance, the Nevada Theatre was jammed and people climbed into trees and onto houses to get a glimpse and give a hearty cheer as "little Wixy" passed by.

Needless to say, Emma's performance, which was concluded with "The Last Rose of Summer," was greeted with a wildly cheering but misty-eyed audience.

Although Emma's later life was marred by many tragedies, she did realize a lifelong dream when her daughter Mignon, whom she and she alone had trained, made her successful operatic debut in Rome in 1910 and went on to also gain acclaim as a world-renowned singer. During the same year, Emma retired from the stage.

Much of Emma's wealth was slowly eroded in seeking a cure for her husband's lingering illness before his death in 1936. Even before this, the American stock market crash had wiped out much of their savings. After her retirement, Emma eked out a living giving music and voice lessons.

Emma's last performance was given in Berlin in 1910. She died near Liverpool, England of natural causes at the age of 81 in June 1940. At the time, the Germans were bombing London.

The Rise and Fall of
HYDRAULIC MINING

It's "the pits," literally.

The remains of the largest hydraulic mining operation in the world, located in the Malakoff Diggins State Historic Park, is a 1600-acre gigantic pit 7000 feet long, 3000 feet wide, and almost 600 feet deep.

A nineteenth century writer called it a "terrible blot on the face of nature" created by forces that were the "very devil's chaos."

It really isn't all that bad now. Nature and time have healed most of the ugly scars and created a mysterious landscape of colorful minarets and spires that are serene and starkly beautiful. And the forces that dug the pit were not supernatural but water combined with man's ingenuity and his desire to get the gold out of the hills and into his "poke."

Water and gold mining in California went hand-in-hand from the beginning.

In 1850, when the streams were nearly picked clean of nuggets, miners near Nevada City discovered gold in ancient riverbeds high above the streams. The problem was how to get water and the high-and-dry gold-bearing ledges together so the gold could be washed out.

At first, miners dug out the ore and hauled it down to streams for washing. Later, they built miles of pipes, ditches, and flumes to carry water to the ledges. But by 1853, they had learned to feed water under pressure through canvas hoses with nozzles to knock the rich gravel from the hillsides into their sluice boxes. Hoses and nozzles rapidly grew longer and larger and capable of delivering more and more powerful jets of water.

The stream from some could hurl a 50-pound boulder with the force of a cannon ball and kill a man more than 200 feet away.

Many small hydraulic mining companies began working the area around North Bloomfield in 1853.

In 1866, a group of capitalists from San Francisco incorporated the North Bloomfield Gravel Mining Company. The Company purchased about 1500 acres near the Malakoff settlement, close to North Bloomfield, and began a large hydraulic operation known as the Malakoff Diggins.

By 1876, the Malakoff Diggins covered more than 1600 acres and went as deep as 400 feet. Twenty-four hours a day, seven days a week, the mountains surrounding the ever-widening mine pit were blasted with water under high pressure through nozzles—called monitors or giants.

The monitors at Malakoff washed away about 50,000 tons of gravel daily and consumed about 16 million gallons of water a year. The water, which was brought to the mine through a canal 45 miles long, came from a reservoir built of wood and rocks containing one billion cubic feet of water.

By 1880, the Malakoff Diggins had become an unequaled giant among hydraulic mining operations. About 60 white men and 40 Chinese were employed in the mine, and from 10 to 30 men worked along the ditch that carried water to the mine site.

Between 1866 and 1884, the Malakoff operation excavated about 41 million yards of earth, which yielded about $3 million in gold, or between five to ten cents per cubic yard.

At the peak of such hydraulic operations in California, thousands of miles of man-made ditches, flumes, and pipelines carried billions of gallons of water to hundreds of hydraulic mines. All of these mines were dumping millions of cubic yards of debris or "slickens" into creeks and rivers.

Results downstream were disastrous.

Periodic floods buried thousands of acres of rich farmland in mining debris and destroyed millions of dollars worth of property and crops.

A survey in 1878 indicated that at least 18,000 acres of once fertile farmland along the Yuba River had been buried under tons of mining debris. Locally, Greenhorn Creek was clogged beneath 200 feet of mining gravel.

Hydraulic mining at Malakoff Diggins.

Marysville, Sacramento, and other river towns had to build miles of costly levees. River traffic was curtailed when mining debris reached as far as the San Francisco Bay. Eventually, only small boats could navigate the Sacramento River.

Although the miners claimed that the "slickens" were good for the farmlands, farmers and "flatlanders" grew sick of too much "slickens" and organized the Anti-Debris Association and took their case to court. In a long series of court battles, flatland farmers were pitted against mountain miners.

Lorenzo Sawyer, a lawyer who was to make the final decision, first came to Nevada County in October 1850. He stayed a short time then moved to San Francisco. He later returned to Nevada County where he practiced law from 1851 to 1853.

During this time, he was one of the lawyers who rushed out of the court house to see the Jenny Lind Theatre washed away by Deer Creek in March 1852.

He also successfully defended "Old Harriet," a "public woman" who kept a saloon near Deer Creek. Harriet and her "fighting man"—bouncer—were accused of murdering Pat Berry who had last been seen alive at Harriet's saloon before he was discovered days later naked and dead in Deer Creek with a savage wound on his head.

The prosecution contended that Harriet and her "man" had smashed Berry over the head, stripped and robbed him, and thrown him in the creek.

Lawyer Sawyer contended that Berry had been slightly drunk when leaving the saloon late at night and had simply fallen off the narrow log that served as the bridge over Deer Creek, struck his head, and drowned.

While the judge was still considering the case, another man, who had accidentally fallen off the same log, was found dead in Deer Creek with most of his clothing ripped off and a similar wound on his head. The judge found "Old Harriet" and her "fighting man" not guilty. Some claim that the success of this case launched Sawyer on his successful career as a lawyer. This seems unlikely as Sawyer had practiced law for a year in Chicago and for three years in Wisconsin before coming to California.

After returning to San Francisco, Sawyer was elected City Attorney. In 1863 he was elected to the California Supreme Court, and he became Chief Justice in 1867. In January 1870, he became the first United States Circuit Court Judge for the West Coast.

Ironically, it was in this capacity that Judge Sawyer was to hand down the decision in the hydraulic case of Woodruff (a Marysville property owner) vs. the North Bloomfield Gravel Company.

When Judge Sawyer came back to the area in late 1882 and early 1883 to inspect the hydraulic mines to get "personal knowledge" of the problems caused to farmlands and waterways by mining debris, he was first snowed out by the biggest snow storm of the season and

then later rained out by the "wettest and best rainstorm of the season."

Miners were delighted. Some declared that the Judge was a "weather breeder" and would be a good man to have around during a drought. (Sawyer did seem to be closely connected with water.)

However, Sawyer had the last word when he handed down his decision on January 7, 1884 in which he declared it illegal for hydraulic mines to dump their debris into streams and rivers. That decision essentially buried hydraulic gold mining.

Although the mines could continue to operate if their debris was properly stored, the cost of building dams to impound such waste was expensive and some of the dams—built only of stone and wood—broke, destroyed valuable mining equipment, and buried rich diggings. Hydraulic miners claimed that some of the dams were deliberately destroyed by anti-hydraulic mining factions.

Legal hydraulic mining virtually ceased; but illegal hydraulicking continued for a time with a network of spies to alert the miners either through quick-riding messengers or over the long distance telephone. Whenever someone suspected of being a Federal inspector arrived in town—they could easily be spotted by their high stiff collars, black suits, and brief cases—word went out to "Shut off the water and tie down the monitors. The 'Feds' are coming."

When the inspector arrived at a hydraulic mine, the ground would be soaking wet even on a hot summer day; but all would be peaceful and quiet with neither miners nor monitors working.

Eventually, even this illegal method proved unprofitable, and all hydraulic mining stopped.

At a visit to the Malakoff Diggins State Historic Park you can still see the remains of this brief period that not only changed the geographic face of the area, but began to shift the state's economic base from gold mining to farming.

GO, GO WASHOE!

By 1853, the pell-mell rush of the 49ers had passed its peak and thousands of unlucky miners who never struck it rich in California began to spill out into Oregon, British Columbia, Arizona, South Dakota, and New Mexico—to any new mining frontier where they could still hear the faint siren song of "Gold!" Others went home or stayed in this area and became hard-rock or hydraulic miners.

Any little rumor could set off a stampede: a new shaft sunk, a tunnel extended, a piece of machinery brought in, a smile on a miner's face, a full "poke," a report in a paper, or, more importantly, a reliable assay.

When James J. Ott opened an assay office in Nevada City and Melville Attwood established one in Grass Valley, they set themselves up smack in the middle of what was to become the richest gold mining area in California. Their locations also brought them unexpected and important roles in assaying one of the richest mineral strikes in the history of the world.

In the early 1850s, rumors leaked over the Sierra Nevada into California that gold had been found in the Washoe country, which was then Utah Territory. A few prospectors trekked over the mountains to see what they could see. Reports came back of miners grubbing laboriously in the hot, arid, windy desert highlands on Sun Mountain—later named Mount Davidson—and sometimes grappling $5 of gold from the recalcitrant mountain in a day. Such prospects didn't attract many miners.

Then in 1859, news came that a comparatively rich outcropping of gold had been discovered in the area. However, the deposits were difficult to work because of lack of timber and water and a

Melville Attwood.

James J. Ott (Courtesy of Mrs. Beatrice Ott Hoge).

blue-black sand that constantly clogged the riffles of the miner's rockers and long toms. The miners stoically worked their claims, cursed the "damned blue stuff," and threw it away as a worthless nuisance.

In late June 1859, John Stone picked up some of the ore containing the curious blue-black material and brought it to Nevada City. Specimens of the ore were passed from friend to friend. Some was given to James J. Ott, and some to Melville Attwood.

They both announced that the ore specimens were not only rich in gold, but exceedingly rich in silver.

On July 1, 1859, the *Nevada Journal* of Nevada City carried the first newspaper report of the assay in a short notice that said Ott's specimen assayed at $840 a ton in "ordinary mill," leaving $130 in "tailings." The ore also had a large quantity of antimony and about $40 in copper to the ton.

Historians say another sample was assayed at $1595 of gold and $3196 of silver to the ton.

As the news spread, the siren song of "Gold!" was quickly drowned by the cry of "Silver! Silver in Washoe!"

Prospectors, miners, adventurers, and investors from this area were among the first to stampede to the soon-to-be-christened Comstock Lode to stake claims. At the head of the pack was George Hearst, a local mine owner, who grabbed a mule and headed over the mountains to buy interests in two of the richest claims before the owners learned of the value of the ore.

Californians by the thousands surged closely behind.

Just as the small nugget of gold discovered at Sutter's sawmill led to the gold rush of 1849, the small bag of ore assayed in Nevada County ten years later started the great Washoe Silver Rush of 1859. One brought hordes of miners into the area, the other almost emptied the area—temporarily.

The silver and gold taken from the Comstock Lode financed much of the Civil War for the North, brought the state of Nevada into the Union, and made millionaires of a lucky few—including George Hearst, John Mackay, James Fair, William O'Brien, and James Flood, who used their wealth to build lordly mansions, palatial hotels, and plush bank and office buildings in San Francisco and string telegraph lines across the continent and cables under the sea.

When the Washoe country was admitted to the Union in October 1864 as the state of Nevada, President Lincoln acquired the two Senate votes he needed to pass the 13th Constitutional Amendment, which freed the slaves.

A COOL DUEL

Disputes between early citizens of Nevada County were usually settled immediately with pistols, knives, or fists. However, a few elected to settle their quarrels in an "honorable" duel.

The Lundy-Dibble duel in 1851 was not "honorable" and it ended in the tragic death of Dibble when Lundy shot before the proper signal was given. However, the results of other early duels were more often comic than tragic, as precautions were sometimes taken to make sure that the duelists would survive with both their honor restored and their skin intact.

In 1853, as duelists Billy Mason and H. C. Gardiner took pot shots at each other while darting in, out, and around buildings, a large crowd gathered to watch the outcome from a safe distance. When the pistols were emptied and the smoke of battle had cleared, the results were: "two calves and a pig." Each of the duelists had been shot in the calf of his leg, and a pig that blindly rushed into the middle of the battleground was killed by a stray bullet.

In 1860, Captain J. B. Van Hagan and R. B. Moyes decided to settle their dispute with "minnie rifles" at 60 paces. At the "word," both fired—and both missed. Each demanded another shot. A sarcastic bystander suggested that they put telescopes on their rifles so they could see each other. After the heckler was silenced, the duelists fired again—and missed again. Since they couldn't reach each other with "minnie rifles," they worked out their differences with a "big talk" and retired from the field of honor with honor.

In North Bloomfield in 1866, Souchet and Picard, two Frenchmen, elected to salve their wounded honors in a duel with pistols at 25 paces. Their attendants thoughtfully furnished each contestant with a pistol loaded with a "ball" only. When the duelists snapped their "caps" at each other and discovered the fraud, they demanded different pistols.

Steps were again paced off, and the antagonists emptied their pistols at each other with no better results. Infuriated, Souchet advanced on Picard and smashed him over the head with the empty gun. Picard quickly retreated—somewhat battered but alive.

The next day, they were both arrested for assault and for fighting to the "great terror" of the citizens of California and North Bloomfield. Picard's honor was somewhat mollified when he served only 20 days in jail to Souchet's 21.

During a Christmas eve ball near Cherokee in 1874, the town blacksmith and Mr. Wall got into a dispute over who got to dance with the same charming lady. The blacksmith threatened to pound Wall into the floor. Wall resented the proposal and challenged the blacksmith to a duel.

Bright and early on Christmas morning the antagonists met on Badger Hill and paced off 30 feet. The blacksmith fired first and missed. Wall, being a stalwart gentleman, pointed his pistol skyward and fired. The contestants then shook hands and swore eternal friendship. Neither had ever been in danger as their seconds had carefully left out the bullets.

No one seems to know what caused the dispute that arose in July 1861. Some surmised that A. B. Carley had insulted E. O. Tompkins' sausages. Others thought Tompkins had made a derogatory remark about Carley's cocktails. For whatever reason, when Tompkins demanded satisfaction, Carley accepted the challenge.

As word of the impending duel spread, excitement ran high.

In accordance with custom, Carley had the honor of selecting the time, place, and the weapons. Commercial Street in Nevada City was set as the place and 3 p.m. as the time. Nat Browne, editor of the *Nevada Daily Transcript,* and Mr. Tower, a Wells, Fargo agent, were selected as seconds.

A large crowd awaited anxiously as the duelists and their seconds marched onto the battleground.

Carley in a red shirt and plug hat and Tompkins in a blue shirt and slouched hat stood face-to-face—25 feet apart.

They both had fire in their eyes, but no one knows what was in their hearts as they defiantly fingered their formidable weapons

At a signal, each combatant carefully took aim.

At the word of "Fire!" each was instantly smashed with the full force of 150 pounds of water pressure shooting out of a 25-foot hose equipped with a quarter-inch nozzle.

The first to fall was Carley's plug hat. But Carley fought back valiantly.

When the order of "Right and Left!" was shouted, the combatants turned their weapons on the crowd, causing a soggy stampede.

When Mr. Tower, no longer content to be a mere second, jumped into the fracas and grabbed Tompkins' weapon, he fought heroically until his hose "busted." The contest was then called off. Everyone left the field of battle dripping with good fellowship and honor washed clean, but not before the combatants vowed to renew the duel with larger nozzles.

Whether they did or not is not known. It is known, however, that such hydraulic duels are still an important part of Fourth of July parades in Nevada County. Perhaps the beautifully coiffured ladies who are sometimes surprised by these duels would like to know a historical precedent for such frivolity so they could hang Tompkins and Carley in effigy over a nearby beauty shop.

The Rise and Fall of
THE SUSPENSION BRIDGE

Many early bridges in Nevada County were neither beautiful nor safe. Several collapsed under heavy loads or were washed away by raging winter floods.

One of the worst disasters happened early on the morning of July 10, 1862 when the people in Nevada City were awakened by a terrifying crash. Hundreds rushed toward the foot of Pine Street to discover a tragic scene of death and destruction.

The recently completed suspension bridge on Pine Street over Deer Creek had collapsed hurling two teamsters, two wagons loaded with hay, and two teams of oxen into the creek bed 50 feet below.

The two young teamsters, their dog, and 12 of 18 oxen were killed.

Although two men who were crossing the bridge on foot at the time of the catastrophe scrambled to safety, a third was hurled into the creek bed and severely injured.

It was later determined that a defective piece of iron had snapped, causing supporting iron rods to give way.

The bridge, which had been built at a cost of $9000 and hailed as the most permanent and most useful public improvement in the county, was now a most "melancholy" sight.

Over the protest of many local citizens, Nevada City had levied a property tax of five-eighths of one percent to raise money to build the new bridge to replace one that had become "demoralized by service." The contract was let to a San Francisco firm in October 1861. However, unusually heavy winter rains hampered construc-

Suspension bridge in Nevada City.

tion, and the bridge was not completed and opened to traffic until May 1862.

Although the bridge was no rival to the later San Francisco Bay suspension bridge, it was considered to be a technical marvel and beauty at the time. It boasted a span of 320 feet and was 14 feet wide with suspension towers that rose to a height of 33 feet. Inscriptions bearing the names of the builders were prominently and proudly displayed on each of the suspension towers.

Although two law suits were brought against Nevada City after the bridge fell, neither the city nor the builders were held responsible.

The damage was repaired and the bridge was reopened for traffic in September. It served well until 1904 when it was replaced by the less attractive steel bridge that still stands.

In 1867, the contractor, Andrew S. Halladie, apparently having gained much valuable information from his experience in Nevada City, patented his wire rope suspension bridge. He also went on to gain fame as the inventor of the world-renowned San Francisco cable cars.

THE MAKING OF A MYTH
John Rollin Ridge and Joaquin Murietta

When John Rollin Ridge, a local newspaper editor, died in Grass Valley on October 5, 1867, he was eulogized as one of the most talented writers in California.

Mark Twain, Bret Harte, and Joaquin Miller, his contemporaries, have had many biographers. John Rollin has none and is now virtually forgotten. And yet his life had all the elements of a rattling good story.

John Rollin Ridge's grandfather, Major Ridge, was a Cherokee warrior, an influential tribal chieftain, and an orator of distinction. He owned black slaves, operated the finest plantation in the Cherokee Nation, and adopted the dress and manners of a prosperous Southern planter.

In 1818, Major sent his eldest son, John (John Rollin's father), to Cornwall, Connecticut to be educated. There John fell in love with Sarah Northrup, a young white girl, and threw the people of Cornwall into a state of collective shock. "Outrage!" cried the press and the pulpit.

But John won out over the objections of both the indignant whites and his disappointed parents, who wanted John to marry the daughter of a chief. In 1824, Sarah and John were married. On March 19, 1827, John Rollin Ridge was born on his grandfather's estate near what is now Rome, Georgia.

As white settlers moved into the Cherokee territory, which in-

John Rollin Ridge (seated, left end) with the Cherokee delegation to Washington D.C. in 1866 (Courtesy of California State Library).

cluded parts of North Carolina, Tennessee, and Georgia, they became eager to force the Indians out. With the increasing intrusion of the whites, some Cherokees secretly ceded their land and migrated West. Each cession aroused great resentment among the Cherokees.

When gold was discovered in the Cherokee country of Georgia in 1829, more whites poured into the area. They raided, pillaged, and squatted on Indian homesteads.

To make the Indians' position even more precarious, the State of Georgia declared Cherokee laws invalid and decreed that Indians could not testify against white men in Georgia courts or dig for gold on their own land. Large sections of Cherokee land were annexed to Georgia and any Cherokee who tried to stop other Cherokees from migrating was to be arrested and imprisoned. The U.S. government refused to refute the Georgia laws and repeatedly urged the Cherokees to emigrate to Arkansas.

When John and Major Ridge finally realized the futility of the

Cherokees' situation, they reluctantly decided that the Cherokees should make the best bargain they could with the U.S. and move to Arkansas where many of their brothers were already located. John Rollin's idyllic childhood as heir to wealthy and respected tribal chiefs ended when his father and his grandfather signed the Treaty of New Echota in December 1835.

The Cherokee constitution declared death as the penalty for the sale of any tribal lands. But the Ridges and their supporters agreed to the removal of the Cherokees from their Eastern ancestral lands in exchange for extensive land in the West and $4,500,000.

Major Ridge said as he reluctantly signed the treaty, "I have just signed my death warrant." The treaty split the Cherokees into two feuding factions. The Ross faction blamed the Ridge faction for all the suffering and death the Cherokees later endured along the Trail of Tears.

In the early morning hours of June 22, 1839, twenty-five Cherokees quietly surrounded John Ridge's new home in the Oklahoma Indian Territory. Three forced open a door, entered John's bedroom, and aimed a pistol at John's head as he slept. The pistol failed to fire.

Ridge awakened and fought furiously as they dragged him into the yard. As Sarah, John Rollin, and the other Ridge children watched, several men held Ridge by the arms and body while another stabbed him 25 times and then slit his throat. They threw John's dying body into the air. After it fell, all 25 stomped over it in single file.

The scene darkened John Rollin's mind with "an eternal shadow."

On the same day, other bands ambushed and killed John Rollin's grandfather and uncle. Fearing for their lives, Sarah took her five children and fled to Arkansas.

John Rollin spent his adolescence in Arkansas. As a teenager he wrote about a "deep-seated" desire for revenge.

In 1841, John Rollin went to college in New England where he proved to be an able scholar and a natural leader. In 1847, he returned to Arkansas and married Elizabeth Wilson, a white woman from Fayetteville.

He soon returned to Indian Territory and joined in a guerrila war against the Ross faction. When Judge David Kell mutilated John Rollin's prize stallion, John killed Kell in self-defense. Since John didn't believe he would get a fair trial before a Cherokee court, he fled to Missouri.

In 1850, John Rollin came to California to seek his fortune. Like many before him, he soon gave up gold mining and turned to writing. As "Yellow Bird," a translation of the Indian name given to him by Major Ridge, he gained recognition as a forceful writer and a talented poet. Many of his articles and poems were published in the *Golden Era* and the *Hesperian,* which were popular magazines of the time.

Later he became an outspoken editor for newspapers in San Francisco, Marysville, Sacramento, Red Bluff, and Weaverville.

In 1864, he became part owner and editor of the *Grass Valley National.*

John Rollin was a fighting editor when editors fought not only with their pens, but with fists, pistols, knives, canes, and occasionally, beer mugs.

During the Civil War, Ridge was a Copperhead and vigorously anti-Lincoln. His fiery editorials supported the Southern cause, but he was one of the few California editors who denounced secession as treason and urged the government to resist it with force if necessary.

A political brouhaha soon developed between Ridge as editor of the *Grass Valley National,* which supported the Democratic presidential candidacy of McClellan, and Blumenthal of the *Grass Valley Union,* which supported Lincoln's re-election. Charges of bribery and chicanery were exchanged. Ridge challenged Blumenthal to a duel, but Blumenthal ignored it. Infuriated, Ridge, along with two friends, entered the *Grass Valley Daily Union* office and caned Blumenthal soundly.

A Marysville paper hooted in mock acclaim at the "bravery of three men who went at midnight to horsewhip a single, unarmed man."

Despite his fiery temper and his virulent pen, when Lincoln was assassinated, Ridge joined Blumenthal in mourning.

His success as an influential political writer and a talented poet in California never dispelled Yellow Bird's yearning to be restored as a chief among his own people and to avenge the wrongs done to his relatives and his tribe.

One of his greatest desires was to establish a paper in the Cherokee Nation where through the "fire of my pen" and the help of the best minds of the Indian nations they would prevent men and governments from trampling on the rights of the defenseless Indian tribes.

John Rollin Ridge (Courtesy of California State Library).

John Rollin never realized these ambitions.

In 1866, he went to Washington with a delegation of the Ridge faction in a last attempt to regain his tribal status. He failed and returned to his home in Grass Valley defeated and depressed. He died soon after at the age of 40 and was buried in the Greenwood Cemetery on West Main Street near Grass Valley.

The poetry John Rollin wrote in his youth was published in a slender volume after his death. It received short and limited literary acclaim.

Ironically, when John Rollin was 27, he wrote a romanticized tale about another man's life that became one of the West's most enduring legends. In his book *The Life and Adventures of Joaquin Murieta, the Celebrated California Bandit,* John Rollin portrays Murietta as a peaceful and noble citizen who is transformed into a bloody outlaw dedicated to revenging the atrocities he and his family suffered at the hands of white men.

In the book, Murietta gets the revenge that John Rollin longed for. (Murietta and his gang killed quite a few white men.) Murietta lives on in poems, articles, books, plays, in old movies and recent television programs. John Rollin's story of Murietta is the main source from which many of these later accounts came.

But history has taken little note of John Rollin Ridge, the man known as Yellow Bird.

THE NEVER COME, NEVER GO
and How She Came and Went

One of Nevada County's most written about, talked about, and beloved celebrities was neither a bewitching paramour-danseuse like Lola Montez nor a brilliant philosopher-historian like Josiah Royce but a short, small, clinking, clanking, smoke- belching, and whistle-screeching railroad—the Nevada County Narrow Gauge Railroad (NCNGRR).

The NCNG—affectionately nicknamed the "Never Come, Never Go"—had a lot going for it—high trestles and bridges, steep grades, sharp curves, tunnels, and picturesque scenery that included rich gold mines, bustling lumber mills, wild canyons, cultivated valleys, roaring rivers, and teeming streams.

The NCNG not only carried people, it carried lumber, merchandise, heavy mining machinery, apples and peaches, dynamite and gold—all of it together.

It also transported theatrical troupes and circuses and large crowds to local picnics, political rallies, holiday celebrations, and on moonlight excursions to lovely downtown Colfax.

Throughout its history, local papers reported every phase of the exciting "saga" of the NCNG from conception through construction to completion and final destruction.

During 1874 and 1875 local papers reported on the progress of the railroad as the road was surveyed, contracts were let, men were

*The Never Come, Never Go
crossing the Bear River trestle.*

hired, buildings were moved, trees were blown up, tunnels were blasted, bridges and trestles were built, track was laid, and engines and rolling stock arrived.

On January 17, 1876, the engine named "Grass Valley" steamed into the Grass Valley station for the first time. The locomotive gave a long whistle, which was answered by the bell of the Protection Hose Company.

Despite the sharp wind and cold weather, a large crowd of Nevada County's "best citizens" celebrated the "road getting in." A jubilant supper party for the public was held by the ladies of Grass Valley at Hamilton Hall, and the headlights of the "Grass Valley" engine illuminated the way to the festivities.

Construction toward Nevada City proceeded at less than a lightening pace. Blizzards, torrential rains, washouts, cave-ins, and first a lack of railroad ties—then spikes—then bolts—then straps—delayed the extension of the track to Nevada City.

A rain and snow storm dampened the people but not the spirit of the Completion Day celebration, which finally arrived on May 20, 1876.

The Nevada Light Guard in their "splendid uniforms" along with the Nevada City Fire Department, a brass band, and local dignitaries marched to the depot where more than 1000 people crowded around.

Both the "Nevada" and "Grass Valley" engines arrived with loads of cheering passengers. Bells of the city pealed. Whistles of the mills, machine shops, and the two locomotives shrilled. A cannon thundered from Sugar Loaf Hill, and the people cheered and cheered.

The last tie painted blue with gold edges was set in place. With a sure stroke, John Coleman, the president of the company, drove in a "golden spike" made of polished steel.

Then Judge Niles Searls mounted the "Nevada" engine and gave a "happy speech" in which he presented the NCNGRR to Nevada County as our nation's centennial gift.

After the ceremonies, many of the mud-spattered and rain-bedraggled but happy crowd—soon to get happier—headed for local bars to toast the completion of the railroad.

No doubt the general public loved the Never Come, Never Go for the sheer pleasure it gave as it carried them on all kinds of special outings.

Each year, usually in May—or whenever fair weather returned—a grand picnic was held at the Storms' Ranch picnic ground, which was close to the railroad tracks near what is now Chicago Park.

The combined Sunday Schools picnics and the Miner's Union picnics were also held there annually. Smaller picnics were held at Shebley's pond, also on the rail line, where fun-seekers could not only boat and swim but buy draft beer.

For several years circuses came annually to the area over the NCNG. And special trains went to meet General Grant's train in October 1879, Teddy Roosevelt's train in May 1903, and Herbert Hoover's train in 1932 as they passed through Colfax.

But all was not always picnics and presidents or circuses and cakes on the Never Come, Never Go.

During winter months, snow and heavy rains often crushed tunnels, cut embankments, washed away roadbeds, and caused slides that stalled or blocked trains for hours and sometimes several days.

Fires also destroyed and damaged depots, locomotives, shops, equipment, and bridges. And there were accidents and lawsuits.

Shebley's pond.

The Never Come not only valiantly fought through all these problems but through changes of ownership and being operated several years by a woman.

Before he died in 1901, John F. Kidder, who had become president of the NCNG in 1884, signed over his shares of railroad stock to his wife, Sara, who with the help of C. P. Loughridge, ran the railroad efficiently and honestly for 12 years.

The NCNG survived it all: winter storms, destructive fires, tragic wrecks, and changes of ownership only to be done in by so-called progress combined with World War II.

When revenues fell because of increasing competition from highway transportation and the slowdown of gold mining operations during World War II, the NCNG officially stopped operation in 1942.

The NCNG was taken apart like it was put together—piece by piece. However, the big, beautiful steel bridge over the Bear River that was built in 1908 still stood as a reminder of the heydays and happy days of the railroad until August 1963 when it was to be blasted down to make way for the Rollins Dam project.

Once again, the Never Come, Never Go proved to be—unpredictable. Her last performance was a classic.

A crowd of about 200 devotees gathered for one last look at the remains of their beloved celebrity. After the speeches by the dignitaries were over, a warning whistle shrilled. The project manager dramatically intoned the countdown: "Five, four, three, two . . ." Cameras clicked and whirred. As the final whistle shrieked, a lady pushed down the plunger on the firing box.

At the roar of two mighty blasts of dynamite, a cloud of dust rose from the base of the bridge. The crowd strained to get a better look. The bridge lifted slightly then with a shrug and shudder settled back down just slightly off-center.

As the dust cloud settled, the stunned silence was shattered by shouts of laughter. The stubborn bridge that had stood for 55 years refused to go down.

A bulldozer was called in to attack the bridge. As the dozer strained against a cable attached to the bridge, the cable snapped.

Later in the day, the "demolition experts" blasted off another shot of dynamite. The bridge grudgingly gave up two sections but most of the bridge remained intact and only slightly askew.

Another blast was fired. Nothing happened.

At that point, a red-faced workman whispered to the boss that they were out of dynamite. The workmen were dismissed.

But progress was not to be halted for long. The next day the bridge was cut up with acetylene torches and knocked down by tractors and bulldozers.

The Never Come, Never Go was finally gone. But forgotten? Never!

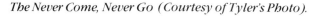

The Never Come, Never Go (Courtesy of Tyler's Photo).

HOW TRUCKEE
—a Wild and Wooly Railroad-Lumber Town—
GOT RESPECTABLE

The Name

In the fall of 1844, a group of emigrants stopping at the Humboldt Sink before attempting to cross the treacherous high Sierra was greeted by a Paiute Chief who repeatedly called out "tro-kay, tro-kay"—meaning everything is all right—to let them know that he was peaceful. The emigrants mistakenly thought the Chief was telling them his name was Truckee. So when the Chief obligingly showed the emigrants a pass through the Sierra that followed a river, they thought they were honoring the Chief by naming the river Truckee.

Although early gold seekers prospected along the Truckee River, the placer pickings were so slim and the winter climate so harsh they quickly moved on to more productive rivers and streams.

The Railroad

Then when the Central Pacific railroad route was laid out over the Sierra, a turnpike that followed the railroad's right-of-way was built between Dutch Flat and the Truckee Basin to be used to haul in railroad supplies.

The first settlers to arrive in the present-day location of Truckee were Joseph Gray and his family. In 1863, Gray built a log cabin near the turnpike. The location was known as Gray's Station as the cabin also served as a station for stages, teamsters, and travelers.

Later, Mr. Coburn, another early settler, built more buildings to accommodate the increasing stream of people, provisions, and supplies that passed through to the Washoe mines in Nevada; and the name of the place was changed to Coburn's Station.

In 1868, men building the Central Pacific railroad began to arrive in the area, and a bustling town—providing the usual necessities of saloons, stores, and lodgings—sprung up around Coburn's Station.

Lumber

Several sawmills were also built in the area to meet the increasing demands for lumber for mine construction in Washoe and for construction of the railroad as it crept into the Sierra.

In July 1868, Coburn's Station went up in smoke, but another town was quickly rebuilt nearby and renamed Truckee. The town soon earned a reputation as a wild and wooly railroad and lumbering town where the liquor ran freely, gambling was nonstop, shootings, brawls, and brouhahas were frequent, most of the ladies were "professionals" in "hurdy-gurdy" houses, and the men worked like mules to earn the money they spent like asses.

After 1868 when the railroad pushed through the mountains, Truckee became the main town on the railroad line between Sacramento and Ogden, Utah. Lumber in various forms from huge logs and thin shingles to boxes and charcoal was soon being shipped throughout the country.

But "bad" men and "fallen" women who settled in Truckee created a "great deal of trouble" and caused a "constant uneasiness." That feeling of "uneasiness" nearly earned Truckee a reputation to rival Downieville's.

In 1871 after a violent all-day argument in their downtown Truckee saloon, Mr. Louis Derr informed Mrs. Derr that he was leaving and "never coming back." To make sure he kept his vow, Mrs. Derr set fire to the saloon. The fire spread rapidly and destroyed 68 buildings and left 63 families homeless.

Irate citizens were in a "hanging" mood, but Mrs. Derr was saved from the fate of Juanita of Downieville—the only woman hanged in California—when she was hurried out of town on the first passing train.

Despite these frequent hot feuds and disastrous fires, the area was also one of the coldest spots in the Sierra, which led to the manufacturing of a most respectable product.

Ice

The ice tinkling in your glass today probably didn't travel but a few feet. But when early 49ers "bellied up" to bars in Sacramento and San Francisco, any ice in their drinks had sailed all the way from Boston or Alaska. And local drinkers never had to worry about ice diluting their "tanglefoot whiskey" in the summertime. That is until 1868, when the Truckee Basin began to be turned into a mammoth ice box.

In 1868, the Boca Mill and Ice Company at Boca—about five miles from Truckee—built a dam and flooded 30 acres to create a pond to float logs into the mill. The ice on the pond was also harvested in the winter and shipped by rail to markets in the lowlands. In 1869, the company built a 40 × 484-foot ice house that was 17 feet high in which 8000 tons of ice could be stored.

Since this operation proved successful and the demand for Truckee ice increased rapidly, more ice companies were formed. Rivers and streams were dammed, hundreds of acres were flooded, and more ice houses were built.

Little settlements consisting of boarding houses, stables, blacksmith shops, and tool houses sprung up around the ice companies.

When the ponds froze, teams of horses, wearing specially designed shoes for walking on ice, pulled ice plows that scribed the ice ponds like gigantic checkerboards. Armies of men with large saws then cut the ice into huge chunks, which were floated down open channels, lifted by steam powered engines or slid by gravity down steel runways, and stacked tier on tier in large ice storage houses.

Each year as much as 300,000 tons of Truckee ice was used to refrigerate California produce shipped to the East and, after 1872, to cool mine shafts in the Comstock Lode. Because of its crystal purity, Truckee ice was also packed in straw and shipped to cool drinks throughout the West Coast and to posh restaurants in New York and New Orleans.

The wooden flumes built to zip logs down the mountains into streams and rivers so they could be floated to lumber mills were often put to other uses—from carrying simple, crude boats loaded

Natural ice being harvested in Boca (Courtesy of Tom Macaulay).

with mail, messages, and supplies to transporting frightened reporters looking for an exciting story or foolhardy loggers in a hurry to get to town.

In 1873, another potential use for the flumes proved to be impractical. When an 11-inch thick block of ice was shot down a 3-mile flume, it arrived at the end as a 3-inch ice cube. The experiment was abandoned.

The profitability of the Truckee ice box gradually melted when artificial ice took over the market in the 1920s.

Sheep, Beef, and Butter

In contrast to the "uneasy" atmosphere that pervaded Truckee, several peaceful pastoral industries thrived in the nearby areas.

In the summertime, sheep, dairy, and cattlemen from the foothills would drive large herds into the Truckee Basin to fatten them on rich high-meadow grasses. Although the land was in the public domain, herders respected each others rights and they would return to the same range year after year.

Each year, about 100,000 to 150,000 sheep would be herded into the Truckee Basin to be fattened, then sheared, so their fleece could be shipped to market from railroad stations in the area before the flocks were driven back to the lowlands in October.

Dairy cows and beef cattle also grazed in the Truckee Basin during the summertime. It was claimed that the beef was neither tender nor juicy because climbing so many hills made the steaks as rough and tough as the badmen of Truckee. But Truckee butter was a highly sought-after product—sometimes for strange reasons.

By the 1880s, Truckee butter was in great demand not only at nearby lumber mining camps but in high-class restaurants and hotels in the valley. And from 15 to 20 dairy farms near Truckee were producing about 60,000 pounds of mountain butter annually.

One of the most unusual demands was discovered by dairyman Joerger who one summer sold all his butter—thousands of pounds—to a single customer.

At a nearby sawmill, logs were moved down a steep incline on tracks called "skids," which were made of logs laid in parallel rows. To get the logs to move down the skids at a good clip, the skids were usually greased with tallow. But when the sawmill owner discovered he was paying less for famous Truckee butter than for tallow, he bought Joerger's entire supply of butter to grease his skids.

It became a local joke for lumbermen to bellow down the table, "Hey, Mac, slide the skid-grease this way. I want to grease my biscuits."

Boca beer label.

Boca Beer

Another of the Truckee Basin's claims to fame was the beer brewed by the Boca Brewing Company. The brewery building, which covered an acre of ground, was completed in 1876. By the late 1870s, more beer was being brewed by the Boca Brewing Company—about 30,000 barrels each year—than in all the other 14 breweries in Nevada County.

Because it was brewed with pure, natural spring water, Boca beer had an excellent nationwide reputation. It was also popular at the World's Fair in Paris in 1883. Unfortunately for beer lovers, the brewery was destroyed by fire in 1893.

Trout and Tourists

Another famous Truckee Basin product was Truckee trout. While tons of succulent native trout were being shipped out, troops of fishermen were being lured in to try their luck in the Truckee River or at Tahoe, Donner, Independence, and Webber lakes.

Over the years, the disreputable atmosphere of Truckee was gradually softened by nearby pastoral scenes of contented dairy cows, peaceful grazing sheep, and the production and shipment of reputable and diversified lumber products, firm and tasty butter, crystalline ice, sparkling beer, and delicious trout.

As people became aware of the beauty of the area, along came the inevitable tourists. Some came to Donner Lake to listen to the brass band while taking a steamboat ride on the *Minnie Moody.* Others came to enjoy the pristine beauty of Lake Tahoe. However, most of these early tourists "snubbed" the rough and tumble town of Truckee. That is until 1893 when Charles McGlashan came up with a "cool" idea that literally stopped tourists on the railroad tracks.

Monster Icicles, Ice Palaces, and Snow Fiestas

Charles McGlashan, a prominent citizen of Truckee, was a man of many talents and many ideas. But this above all: McGlashan was a Truckee booster.

During the winter months of 1893–1894, Truckee slumped into her usual winter doldrums and economic depression. Lumbering and ice harvesting had stopped with the first heavy snowfall. About the only activity for Truckee residents was watching the snow pile

Believed to be the first "monster icicle" built by Charles M. McGlashan in Truckee (Courtesy of Truckee-Donner Historical Society).

up and occasional Southern Pacific (previously the Central Pacific) trains chug through the center of town loaded with passengers gawking at the snowy, scenic beauty of the high Sierra.

That's when McGlashan's idea of a "snow cure" for Truckee's winter woes began to form. Why not give Mother Nature a helping hand and give the passengers on the Southern Pacific something to really gawk at?

McGlashan set to work building a skeleton framework of chicken wire—45 feet high and 10 feet across at the base—near the famed rocking stone in Truckee. Day after day he ran water over the structure. The water quickly froze, and as the ice built up, the icicle grew larger and larger and gradually formed a gigantic 60-foot icicle. McGlashan illuminated his icicle at night with an arc light so it would glimmer and shimmer before the startled eyes of Southern Pacific passengers.

This "monster icicle" fired up local enthusiasm. Why stop with a giant icicle? Why not take advantage of the natural beauty of the Sierra winters—with help from man-made improvements—and attract crowds from the lowlands by offering all kinds of winter sports and attractions and turn winter into a profitable and lively season for local merchants?

In December 1895, the citizens of Truckee were busily building an "Ice Palace," which contained a 700-foot long by 200-foot wide skating rink. Pipes were laid so the palace, ice rink, and large fir trees placed around the roof of the palace could be sprayed with water that would freeze and transform the wooden frame and chicken wire structure into a fairy ice palace.

As word of the Truckee "Ice Palace" spread, heavy snowfall and freezing weather were followed closely by excursion trains with hundreds of people from throughout California, which brought "joy again to Truckee."

According to an eyewitness report, the ice palace was like a "dream of dazzling beauty." The skating gallery had a surface like a great big mirror. Jeweled icicles hanging in clusters from the arched ceiling of the ice gallery sparkled with all the colors of a beautiful rainbow, creating an appearance of "unusual splendor." When the palace was lighted at night, the effect was "extremely grand . . . the like of which can be seen only at the Truckee Ice Palace."

The Ice Palace was again the central tourist attraction in Truckee during the winter of 1896–1897.

After 1897, news of the Ice Palace and winter carnivals in Truckee fades from regional newspapers for several years. Possibly local enthusiasm and support cooled.

In the meantime, skiing was becoming the "rage" in Truckee. To the dismay of many local "doubters," the Chlepp (Clepp, Klepp) brothers, expert skiers, went to the highest peak near Truckee and came down "safely." Following these experts' examples, about a half dozen local people began trying to master the "art of manipulating Norwegian skis."

The Truckee newspaper continued to boost a winter sports carnival, declaring that both tobogganing and skiing had the new "fad" of flying "skinned to a frazzle."

In February 1909, a committee was formed to boost the idea of holding another winter carnival. The committee eventually raised enough subscriptions to hold a carnival on March 6 and 7, 1909. The Truckee paper claimed that it was "the first time in the history

Skiing in the Truckee area in the late 1800s (Courtesy of Truckee-Donner Historical Society).

of the state that such an elaborate program of events" had been arranged.

The fun began with the "merriment of snowballing" and washing the faces of "fair ones" with soft snow as soon as people stepped off the train at 6:30 a.m.

After breakfast, the happy crowd chartered six-horse bobsleds for old-fashioned rides in all directions. The fare for a round trip to Donner Lake was 50 cents.

At 10 a.m., ski jumping began on Snow Peak. Mrs. Gundstrom gave a "pretty exhibition" that showed how easy ski "riding" and jumping was for ladies. (At the time, there were only a few expert skiers in the West, and female skiers were even more rare.)

The "clown from Hobart Mills was a continual scream." Every time he came over the jump he lit on his "left ear," which pleased the onlookers immensely.

Events also included races on Canadian snowshoes, on skis, and on Yankee Jumpers, which were skis made from whiskey barrel staves with a small upright post in the middle with a seat attached.

Toboggans, bobsleds, hand-sleds, and skis were available—all free—which impressed the excursionists.

Two of the great hits were coasting and the Yankee Jumpers.

Waiting in line to enter the Truckee Ice Palace (Courtesy of Truckee-Donner Historical Society).

Although not many "grown-ups" cared to risk their lives on the Yankee Jumpers—those "merciless imps of the snow"—many children did.

The nearby hills were black with toboganners, and the "ski slide" was also dotted with people trying their skill at the new sport. Many failed to land on "the proper place of their anatomy" though they did "hit the ground sooner or later."

Evening dinner between 6:30 and 9 p.m. was followed by moonlight sleighing parties. At 9:55 p.m., the train left for San Francisco.

According to the Truckee paper, from 1910 to 1917 the annual winter carnivals and winter sports facilities in Truckee were increasingly better, larger, and more successful. Promoters continued to boost and boast—claiming that Truckee was fast becoming one of the nation's greatest winter sports areas.

Interesting ice sculptures continued to be a feature of the carnivals. One year, a great arch in downtown Truckee was covered with ice and an icy gate to the town was closed with a gilded padlock, which was ceremoniously opened with a giant key for trainloads of visitors. A direct descendant of the "monster icicle" reappeared in 1913.

Other attractions included all-night dancing, movie companies filming on location, and demonstrations of the rotary snowplow that could toss six- to ten-foot snowbanks from the train tracks.

Unusual "sporting" events included basketball, baseball, and football games, boxing matches, running races, and a catch-a-greased-pig contest—all in the snow.

By 1911, progress began to take its toll as carnival promoters started charging 25 cents for the use of skis and toboggans—whether used for half an hour or half a day.

During carnival time, searchlights, bonfires, and electric lights strung throughout the town and sporting areas turned Truckee's nights into days. Even a large moose head from Reno was strung with lights to greet a Moose organization.

The name of the festivities was changed to the "Fiesta of Snows," and red and white—to represent the holly berry and snow—became the official fiesta colors.

As the fiestas continued to increase in popularity, committees tried to hold carnivals for three months from December 15 to March 15. But snow continued to be both a blessing and a curse. At times, it didn't fall in sufficient amounts until late in the season. At other times, it fell so heavily that it wrecked or temporarily blocked trains, which prevented some visitors from getting in on sched-

A Truckee Ice Palace with an attached toboggan slide (Courtesy of Truckee-Donner Historical Society).

ule—which was bad for business—or out on schedule—which was good for business.

Despite these little drawbacks, people poured into Truckee in greater and greater numbers from throughout California and Nevada.

More and more motion picture companies—including the Famous Players Company with Mary Pickford and the Charlie Chaplin Film Company with Charlie Chaplin—came to Truckee to shoot snow, carnival, and "Alaskan" scenes.

Although dog-sled races were big in Alaska, the Truckee paper claimed that the first Alaskan dog-sled race in California or the United States was held in Truckee in 1915. Participants included John Johnson who was the best dog team driver in the world. Johnson won the Truckee race with his team of Siberian wolves.

In 1916, Jack London and his wife came to see the dog-sled races and "frolic in the snow." By then, Truckee's "Fiesta of Snows" had been given coverage in magazines and newspapers throughout the U.S. Attendance had climbed to between 20,000 and 30,000 annually.

And so the fiestas continued until an increase in automobiles, improved highways, and the development of larger winter sports resorts in the Tahoe area gradually shoved Truckee out of the winter sports spotlight.

Snow did prove to be a temporary cure for Truckee's winter woes. And even now, as millions of skiers buzz to Tahoe in automobiles porcupined with skis, many stop at Truckee for rest or food and leave a few tourist bucks. Yet, probably few of them realize that here is where a "monster icicle" followed by a fantasy Ice Palace, and, eventually, a series of winter carnivals probably gave California winter sports one of its earliest boosts. A boost that undoubtedly helped the Tahoe region become a major California winter sports area.

LYMAN GILMORE'S HIGH FLYING SCHEMES

On December 17, 1903, the Wright brothers achieved the world's first successful powered flight of an airplane at Kill Devil Hill in North Carolina.

Right? Wrong!

Nevada County's Lyman Gilmore, Jr. flew a powered aircraft in May 1902 many months before the Wrights' flight.

That's what Gilmore and others claim. And they go on to contend that Gilmore not only flew before the Wrights, he also established the first commercial airfield in the United States and the first flying field in the West.

At least, that's the legend. But, is it true? Could history be wrong about the Wrights?

Lyman was born June 11, 1874 near Olympia, Washington, the sixth of 11 children.

Like many aviation pioneers, Lyman began his aviation experiments at an early age by building gliders out of just about any material he could lay his hands on.

There's the story about Gilmore and the farmer's flock. It seems a farmer hired Gilmore to take care of a large flock of turkeys for a few days. When the farmer returned he found that the turkeys had mysteriously molted. Gilmore had plucked them and glued the feathers onto a glider—or so the story goes. The feathered glider didn't work, and Gilmore was also out of work. The farmer fired him.

Around 1894, like so many adventurers before him, Gilmore left home when he was 20 and headed for California.

Gilmore's aviation experiments in Nevada County from the 1890s to the early 1900s are clouded by time, lack of solid proof, and Lyman's and reporters' tendencies to tell a good story—regardless of lack of facts. Yet his legend persists.

As happens to many people who come to California, Gilmore had a vision. In 1895 he had a vision of a great airship sailing over hills and mountains carrying happy, smiling people. Gilmore began to design a monoplane patterned after that vision.

The ship was to have a 65-foot wingspan and include such advanced principles as retractable landing gear, a metal covering for the wings and body, and an enclosed, metal eight-passenger cabin.

Some evidence supports this claim. In Lyman's records is a set of plans for the monoplane dated April 27, 1898.

But, according to Gilmore, his big triumph came in 1902 when he built a 32-foot aircraft powered by a steam engine, which he flew successfully in May 1902, about 19 months before the historic flight of the Wrights.

So far, no evidence of the flight—except some of Gilmore's notes—has been found.

Although there is not much evidence to support the stories of Gilmore's early experiments, in August 1909 Gilmore gained the attention of the *Grass Valley Union* newspaper, which declared

The large and small monoplanes built by Lyman Gilmore, Jr., in the early 1900s and the hangar at Gilmore Field.

that "Down at Colfax they boast of a full-fledged aviator, who has made a flight without breaking his neck." They were referring to Gilmore.

Despite the paper's comments on the aviator not breaking his neck, Lyman's brother, Harrison, once told a reporter that during this period it was his job to carry the plane, which had a five-foot wingspan, back up the canyon to Lyman after Lyman had shoved it off a cliff. This statement makes it doubtful the machine was big enough to carry a pilot. Some reports also indicate the plane was guided by remote control.

An old stock certificate states that the Gilmore Airship Company was incorporated in February 1910 and $500,000 worth of stock was being sold at $1 per share to raise money.

Although the dates vary from source to source, sometime between 1905 and 1912 Gilmore had incorporated the Gilmore Airship Company and had established an "airship camp" and workshops and a flying field in Grass Valley—where the Lyman Gilmore School is now located. Many local pilots remember flying in and out of the field, which may well have been the first one in the West. It certainly was *one* of the first.

And although there is no known proof of the exact dates, two monoplanes—one big, one little—were built. Many local citizens remember seeing them in the early 1900s. Gilmore "claimed" he built them in 1903.

In September 1911, Gilmore arranged for a trial flight at his "airship camp."

The test did not go well. Gilmore tied the smaller aircraft to the ground inside his workshop and started the motor to test the engine. Everything was running smoothly when the crankshaft snapped in two and smashed the engine into hundreds of little pieces that were thrown all over the shop.

But did Gilmore give up? Never! This man had the "Right Stuff!"

He ordered another bigger and more expensive engine.

In March 1912, Gilmore tried to fly again—and failed again.

As soon as he started the engine of his small aircraft at Gilmore Field, people by the hundreds came in automobiles and buggies and on bicycles and on foot to watch. They came to see Lyman finally take to the sky. But he didn't. Instead, he roared the small aircraft around the big field for about six hours. Toward the end of the day, a wheel struck a boulder, the plane tipped, struck the ground, and cracked the propeller.

Charles Gilmore (left) and Lyman Gilmore, Jr.

The crowd was disappointed and so were the stockholders, but Gilmore wasn't. He said he had made as much progress as he had expected.

Why didn't the craft fly? Probably because the engine didn't have enough power to lift the heavy machine.

(Way back in 1871, the *Daily National Gazette* of Nevada City predicted that if an aircraft propelling power that weighed "nothing" and "cost nothing" could be devised, man would surely fly. The problem still plagued Gilmore in the 1900s.)

Throughout his years of trials, failures, and misfortunes, Gilmore's vision of the future of aviation never dimmed. And it was practical. He continued to plan and promote an airline service that would link cities and small towns throughout California and the nation. He continued to work on designs of aircraft that would deliver people, mail, and supplies quickly, dependably, and economically. And he predicted that people would soon use aircraft as they then used the automobile.

By the 1920s, Gilmore had begun to be respected and admired as a pioneer of California aviation.

On May 7, 1927, a group of people prominent in aviation attended the Statewide Aeronautical Conference in San Francisco. Along with photographs of some of these dignitaries in the *San Francisco Chronicle* is a photograph of Lyman.

The report states: "Lyman Gilmore, Jr., short of stature, but long of hair and wearing a beard that never had felt a razor, and appearing generally like a person from an age-long past, came unobtrusively into the Aeronautical Convention. . . . Most of those present wondered whence he had come and why he was there. But there were men of long identity with aviation affairs . . . who crowded around to shake Lyman Gilmore, Jr. by the hand.

". . . From those who accorded him such warm welcome it was ascertained that the strange appearing man bears the distinction of being a pioneer aviator and one whose experiments have done much to advance the science of aviation."

But the report doesn't say that Gilmore flew before the Wrights.

Sometime before 1930, Gilmore was presented a certificate from the Daniel Guggenheim Fund for the Promotion of Aviation, which recognized his achievement in "contributing to the establishment of a nationwide system of transportation by air." The certificate is signed by Charles A. Lindbergh.

In the 1930s, Gilmore's hangar and his two experimental aircraft were destroyed by fire. Later, Lyman's home, where most of his records were kept, also burned. Perhaps that is why so much information is missing.

The dreams of Lyman seemed to have gone up in smoke. Then along came a reporter and the legend of Lyman was rekindled by two *Sacramento Union* articles published in June 1935. In these articles, Gilmore recites his many early claims to fame. And this is the legend that appears in most subsequent stories.

As the legend grew, so did Gilmore's fame. In September 1946,

Gilmore was honored by the Nevada City Chamber of Commerce at an aerial circus. In March 1947, his achievements were hailed when Gilmore Field celebrated its 40th birthday. In February 1950, he was feted as an "air pioneer" by the Sacramento Trade Club.

Soon after, on February 18, 1951, death struck. Gilmore's death was covered by local, Sacramento, and San Francisco papers.

On November 2, 1968, the Lyman Gilmore School was dedicated in honor of the "first aviator in California." In 1978, the large mural of Gilmore and events in his life was painted onto one of the school buildings. And so, Lyman continues to soar out of the dim past while historians continue to search for evidence to support his legend.

Did he fly before the Wrights? Some say, "Yes." Others say, "No." From the evidence presently available, it seems doubtful.

But whether Lyman flew before the Wrights or not, many of Gilmore's ideas and designs and his continuous promotion of aviation and a worldwide airline system have proven him to be a true and important aviation pioneer.

AN EMPIRE RESTORED

An Empire has been restored at the Empire Mine State Historical Park in Grass Valley. And the royal couple—the Empire mine and the Bourn cottage—are again officially receiving thousands of visitors each year. If you pay them a call, you can see the splendor that remains of a past age and learn about their interesting history.

The slow rise but long reign of the Empire mine—from 1850 to 1956—paralleled the development of hard-rock mining in California and of Grass Valley as a leading gold-mining community.

Gold-quartz mining has been classified as one of the "most uncertain of all occupations" because not one quartz miner in a thousand ever made even a "moderate fortune."

The Empire mine proved to be the major exception.

Since it took large amounts of capital and large crews of men to sink shafts and dig, haul, and crush the quartz before the gold could be extracted, most early-day gold miners stuck to the placer and hydraulic mining methods.

However, as surface deposits were worked out, some of the more adventurous and hardy miners pock-marked large areas with shallow "coyote" holes and tried their luck at hard-rock mining. Their luck was generally bad.

The inexperience of the miners, the crudeness of the early machinery, and poor management led to many disastrous hard-rock mining failures.

Then things began to change when tin and copper miners from Cornwall, England came to work in the gold-quartz mines and settled in the Grass Valley area during 1852 and 1853. These miners, who were known as the world's greatest hard-rock miners, brought with them invaluable skills and knowledge of hard-rock mining techniques and equipment that contributed greatly to the growing success of hard-rock mines in Nevada County.

By 1861, most of the miners in Grass Valley were Cornishmen.

One of their most valuable contributions was the introduction of the "Cornish pump," a bulky, heavy, outlandish device of iron and wood weighing over 135,000 pounds that meandered deep into the mines to pump out the ground water that constantly accumulated in the mine shafts and hindered operation.

Although the Empire ledge—which was discovered by George D. Roberts in 1850—changed hands many times during these early hard-rock mining days, it continued to prove to be a rich vein.

By 1868, the 30-stamp mill at the Empire, which could crush 40 tons of rock a day, was described as "the most magnificent" mill in California.

But problems continued to plague the mine. In 1870, a fire

A mule pulling an ore cart in the Empire mine (Courtesy of Tyler's Photo).

Miners loaded in skips ready to be dropped into a hard-rock quartz-gold mine (Courtesy of Empire Mine State Historic Park).

destroyed the stamp mill and other surface buildings, equipment, and supplies.

These structures were soon repaired, and in 1871 the Empire was again rated as the "best works in Nevada County."

Between 1854 and 1878, the mine produced around $3 million in gold. However, in 1878, mining experts insisted that the mine was worked out and recommended that it be closed.

William B. Bourn, Jr., the owner's son, disagreed. When he gained control of the Empire in 1877 he reorganized. With the use of the latest in mining technology and equipment and systematic exploration, he again located a rich vein of ore. He then hired his cousin, George W. Starr, an expert mining engineer, as mine superintendent.

Under their efficient management, the Empire mine continued a long, profitable, and successful reign and eventually became a showplace of the latest developments in twentieth century mining techniques and technology.

In 1930 when businesses were failing throughout the nation, the Empire expanded and became the largest gold producer in California. Grass Valley and the miners in the area continued to prosper throughout the depression.

The Empire's mighty reign ended in 1956. With the price of gold fixed at $35 an ounce, the postwar costs for labor, equipment, and supplies made the Empire less profitable to operate than the company's South African mines. The Empire was closed, and much of the machinery and equipment was sold. It appeared that an important part of California history would be lost.

However, in April 1975, the California Department of Parks and Recreation purchased the Empire mine and more than 770 acres of its surface land and buildings, including the Bourn cottage—an architectural showplace.

Today, the mine and the cottage have regained much of their former glory. And on a visit to the Empire, you can take a trip back in time to the heyday of hard-rock mining.

You can peer into the machine, electrical, and carpenter shops and read the placards that explain the use of such mining equipment as Berdan pans, go-devils, stopers, drifters, and Pelton wheels. You can learn that a "coyote whim" is a type of primitive mining operation and not a dog-like animal with a peculiar fancy.

The refinery has a display of the torture-chamber type equipment that was used to put gold through the fiery furnace and mold it into bullion.

You can also inspect the ore carts that hauled tons of ore out of the earth and the skips that three times daily shot crowded loads of men deep into the bowels of the mine.

You can peer down into the lighted mine entrance that bores through a shaft and imagine how it must have been back—when . . .

. . . When miners were loaded 20 at a time into skips and dropped at a speed of about 800 feet per minute down the main shaft with only the feeble light of 20 hand-held candles to illuminate the Stygian underworld.

. . . When the mine owners paid no income tax, and the miners were paid wages of $3.00 a day.

. . . When the people in the area were so accustomed to the constant din of the 24-hour roar of the stamp mill that when the stamps were shut down in 1935 to dig out a miner who had fallen into an ore bin, the entire town was awakened by the sudden silence.

. . . When from 400 to 500 miners worked the vast underground networks of more than 350 miles of tunnels and a series of shafts that reached a collective depth of more than 11,000 feet on the incline.

. . . When 44 mules spent their lives underground pulling ore carts to dumping stations.

. . . When miners had to undress and pass inspection to keep them from "highgrading" (stealing) chunks of gold-bearing ore.

. . . When a mule skinner knew when it was time to skin a mule, literally. After the grieving mule skinner escorted his dead mule past the inspector, he recovered from his grief quickly, cut out his stash of gold from the mule's carcass, and retired—wealthy.

. . . When in over 100 years of almost continuous operation, the miners dug out more than $120 million in gold to make the Empire mine the oldest, biggest, and richest gold mine in the Grass Valley mining district and one of the most famous gold-quartz mines in the world.

The nearby Bourn cottage and grounds show how a small portion of that wealth was spent.

In 1894 William B. Bourn, Jr. commissioned William Polk, a San Francisco architect, to design a "cottage" near the Empire mine. All in all, it is a rather "nice" little cottage where Bourn would stop over when he wasn't at either his San Francisco mansion or his 46-room Filoli estate in San Mateo.

Gold being cleaned out of a bank of stamp mills at the Empire mine.

Although the area looks somewhat like a moderately wealthy English country estate, the unmistakable touch of the gold country is also there.

The wall surrounding part of the grounds was built of rock taken from the Empire mine. In 1913, one of every native tree in California was planted in the area. The sprinkling system for the lawn and for fire protection consists of a series of small monitors whose gigantic cousins were used in hydraulic mining operations to wash away massive hillsides.

The large and impressive shingled building, "The Empire Club," was once the gathering place of the social elite.

Springs under the large dance floor kept the steps of the ballroom dancers light and airy. A tennis court, bowling alley, billiard room, handball and squash courts, and areas for badminton, croquet, and horseback riding kept such visitors as Herbert Hoover and the King of Norway physically fit and happily occupied.

The 12 acres of grounds once required the services of up to ten gardeners who tended 1500 rose bushes and a maze of exotic and native plants and trees. The greenhouse once grew plants that stocked the Golden Gate Park Arboretum.

However, except for special work crews, miners were not allowed on the "cottage" grounds.

THE DAY
THE DAM BROKE

June really "busted out all over" on the morning of June 18, 1883 when the English Dam on the Middle Yuba River broke and unleashed 650 million cubic feet of water. How much water is that? Enough water to build into a gigantic wave 60 feet high that tore along at the rate of 10 miles per hour with a roar that could be heard for miles.

Water stored in the reservoir behind the dam served 80 miles of ditches to hydraulic mine operations in the area.

Fortunately, the dam watchman, George Davis, arrived right after the break and telephoned warnings and approximate times for the arrival of the floodwaters to areas below. These warnings were then relayed by telephone and telegraph and by horseback messengers.

Although there were many narrow escapes and first reports indicated that 30 to 40 people in the San Juan Ridge area had "gone in the flood," final reports generally agreed that only six or seven men had drowned. However, property damages were high as the great rolling wave swept away everything in its path including buildings, houses, cabins, shops, barns, dams, flumes, roads, boulders, trees, sheep, cattle, and mining equipment.

A 200-pound blacksmith anvil was swept away like an autumn leaf in the wind, and huge trees were pounded into splinters.

Just after the Downieville stage crossed the four-span covered Freeman bridge, the bridge was smashed to smithereens. The Oregon Creek bridge was picked up, spun around, and dropped downstream.

A Sacramento Bee cartoon of the damage done by hydraulic mining.

Great sand waves two feet high were tossed into the Feather River and its tributaries. The steamer *Small* got stuck on the sand "slickens" and whistled for assistance from the "snag" boat *Seizer*. *Seizer* started to help the *Small,* but it, too, became stuck in the slickens.

Eighty head of Jim O'Brien's cattle standing in the Yuba River were reluctantly swept away on the "foaming brine" like "Darlin' Clementine," but they eventually clambered back to shore farther downstream.

Miners working in the McKillicon mine escaped being drowned "like rats" by escaping through a recently constructed air shaft as water poured into the mine tunnel.

One reporter said that everything along the river was "wreck and ruin," and in spots "everything was clean gone." Only two bedraggled chickens were left at the Jackson ranch.

Some Chinese who narrowly escaped being swept away in the

flood reported it was the "grandest, most terrible sight, they had ever beheld in all their born days."

When Marysville was warned that the flood waters would reach that area around 2 p.m., a large crowd gathered on the Yuba River bridge to watch the show and place bets on how high the river would rise.

Luckily, a levee broke at the Linda township, and the wall of water spread out over the lowlands like a vast sea, which probably saved the city of Marysville and the disappointed floodwatchers.

Ironically, a *Sacramento Bee* photographer and the president of the Anti-Debris Association, who were inspecting and photographing a brush dam downstream, were saved from being stranded in a wet and dangerous situation when they were warned by a man on horseback who had received the telegraphed warning from their arch-enemies—hydraulic mining men.

Since the English Dam had recently been strengthened and had passed a rigid inspection, many hydraulic mining men believed the anti-mining factions had deliberately destroyed the dam with dynamite. A reward of $5000 for information was never collected, and the cause of the breaking of the seemingly sound dam—especially during a dry month—remained a mystery.

The incident drew statewide attention to the battles that had raged for years—in and out of court—between hydraulic miners in mountain communities and farmers in valley communities.

Valley papers railed at the loss of property and crops that resulted from the flood. Local papers sneered at their accusations and pointed out that the loss of water, flumes, ditches, and mining equipment had thrown more than 100 hydraulic miners out of work and essentially turned French Corral and nearby hydraulic mining communities into instant ghost towns. To local miners, the loss of a few cattle and sheep and the "drowning of a few acres of grain" and a few sections of "swampland" and "bug-eaten soil" in the lower country was "insignificant" and not really serious enough to "wail about."

IS THERE TRUTH
IN ADVERTISEMENT?

Many early California settlers quickly learned that more than one kind of gold could be harvested from the abundant resources, fertile land, and beautiful scenery in Nevada County.

Simmon P. Storms and Joseph Shebley were among the first to recognize that beautiful scenery along with a "gimmick" could pull in people from nearby settlements.

On his extensive ranch, which was once considered to be the "most valuable in the state," Storms not only grew "beautiful" vegetables, melons, poultry, beef, and pork, he built a sporting arena that attracted large crowds to watch and participate in a variety of sports including foot races, wrestling matches, bull and bear fights, and "dog jangling." Hundreds of curious white people came to watch and participate in the sports and to gawk as native Indians in picturesque dress performed ceremonies and dances. Hundreds of Indians came for the sporting events and to gawk at the whites in their picturesque costumes performing their rituals of leisure.

On his acreage, Joseph Shebley established one of the first experimental fish hatcheries in California on Butterfly Creek in the 1870s. His attractive fish ponds were surrounded by vast expanses of lush, green grass in the summertime.

With the completion of the Narrow Gauge railroad between Colfax and Nevada City in 1876, Storms' Ranch and Shebley's ponds became favorite picnic spots for Sunday School children, miners, and all kinds of societies, clubs, and organizations as well as lovers and loafers, fisherpersons and rowboaters.

Other settlers saw the potential profits in supplying fresh fruits and vegetables to nearby settlements. Around 1872, Louis Orzalli established one of the first orchards and vineyards in the vicinity of Shebley's and Storms' acreage—an area that was eventually to become Chicago Park.

By 1886, the Nevada County Promotional Committee was touting Nevada County as a paradise regained. According to their reports, Nevada County offered fertile lands at low prices where "adequate" rainfall could be used for irrigation to produce large and profitable yields of fruits and other farm produce. The climate was hawked as being "temperate" and free of the rigors of Northern winters and the enervating heat of tropical climates.

In the mild climate of Nevada County, farmers could produce two and three crops each year and never have to worry about thunderstorms or sandstorms, tornados or cyclones, malaria or mosquitoes, fogs or floods. The children grew up "plump and firm," and the citizens were intelligent and cultured such as are "found in a modern city."

Both Nevada City and Grass Valley had imposing churches of nearly "all recognized denominations," excellent schools and transportation facilities, large and palatial residences and neat cottages with well-kept lawns and well-cultivated gardens, and large and

Waiting for the Never Come, Never Go at the Chicago Park station in the early 1900s (Courtesy of Ardis Hatten Comstock).

Packing Nevada County fruit in the Chicago Park area.

commodious stores that offered every class of merchandise. The streets of these twin cities were broad, well laid out, and well lighted by gas and electricity.

But lest they seem to oversell this paradise, the Promotional Committee cheerfully admitted that Nevada County wasn't "exactly Paradise," as the weather did have a few "bad aspects," and the fruit in the orchards could be injured by "neglect." And that even in this "glorious climate" people did grow old and die.

One of the grandest early schemes to attract people from outside the state to buy real estate began in 1887 when two men from Colfax convinced a group of investors in Chicago, Illinois to buy about 6700 acres in Nevada County and develop an elaborate townsite near Storms' station on the Narrow Gauge railroad.

Town lots were laid out around a public square, and streets were named after streets in Chicago, Illinois. Large tracts of 10, 20, and 30 acres, called "villas," surrounding the townsite were sold for $75 an acre. Within the townsite, large areas were reserved for an elaborate three-story, 80-room resort-hotel, two churches, an academy, and a large park.

In theory, buyers would built their homes in town and then travel out to work in their paradisal orchards, vineyards, and gardens.

This—the Chicago Park Colony—located in the midst of the "Bartlett Pear Belt of California" and surrounded by the "unlimited resources of the Sierra Nevada foothills"—was promoted through the *Chicago Park Times* newspaper and the *Chicago Park Horticulturist* and was advertised in newspapers in the east, midwest,

Main Street in Grass Valley after a snowstorm in the winter of 1889 and 1890 (Courtesy of Downey Clinch).

and locally. Much of the acreage and lots was sold to people in Illinois and surrounding states.

In 1887, some of the buyers moved to Nevada County and began planting orchards and building fences and a few houses. In March 1889, the assessor declared Chicago Park to be the "most improved section" of the county. However, the town never developed as some of the disgruntled investors refused to back it.

Then in January and again in February of 1890, along came two devilish snowstorms—the greatest snowstorms to hit the area since the coming of the 49ers—and paradise was nearly lost. By the end of the two storms, the seasonal snowfall was about 20 feet.

Crashes were heard throughout the land as the wet, heavy snow crushed houses, caved in roofs, pushed over barns, toppled buildings, knocked down trees, blocked roads and railroads, and isolated settlements.

The few stages that got through during the early part of the storm came in on runners. Eventually sleds, sleighs, and snowshoes were the only means of transportation.

The narrow gauge railroad was blocked for weeks in January and again in February. Tons of mail went undelivered. Malcolm "Doc" McLeon died while trying to help John Grissell deliver mail to Washington on snowshoes.

Supplies and stock dwindled. Even cash became scarce as armies

Joseph Shebley (Courtesy of the Shebley family).

of snowshovelers were paid 30 to 50 cents an hour to shovel snow off roofs and railroad tracks and out of water ditches.

Fortunately for the newcomers in Chicago Park, the more seasoned and experienced Joseph Shebley had laid in a large winter supply that they borrowed until the roads were cleared.

Since the snowflakes, which were jokingly called "Chicago Park orange blossoms," were no joke to many of the colonists, they moved out. As the word drifted back to other buyers, they decided to cancel their trips to paradise.

Although the Chicago Park Colony was considered a failure, other settlers coming into the area developed productive orchards and vineyards. Several of these orchardists contributed pears to the exhibit that took the grand prize at the Panama-Pacific Exposition in San Francisco in 1915.

In time, the Chicago Park area became renowned for its "blushing Bartlett pears." Little did the consumers know that the blush on the pears was really sunburn. But, the pears were delicious, and good advertising can sell just about anything.

LOOKING FORWARD
AND BACKWARD

As Nevada County teetered on the brink of the twentieth century, her citizens looked backward on their 50-year history with great pride and forward to their future with great confidence.

In the *San Francisco Call,* Nevada County "argonaut" Frank Morse recalled his stumbling and bumbling efforts while trying his luck during the early quartz mining experiments in the area. Frank remembered a rattling, banging, chug-chugging wooden steam-operated stamp mill that—when it worked, which wasn't often— could be heard for a mile. To cut down on the noise, the owners, who apparently had no grease, would coat the bearings of the mill with molasses. Morse said he decided to quit mining when his quartz, despite a high yield of $45 to the ton, was costing $50 a ton for crushing.

In early January 1899, the *Grass Valley Union* presented a series of glowing accounts of mine operations in California and Nevada County.

Quartz mining was the most important branch of the mining industry in California followed by placer, hydraulic, and drift mining. In 1898, 19,283 men were employed in the gold, silver, lead, and copper mines in California. Nevada County, the largest gold producing county—about $2.5 million annually—also employed the highest number of men in mining—1949.

This high annual production in Nevada County, which had been maintained for the previous three years, was attributed to the reopening of old mining properties, the discovery of new ones, the increase and improvements in machinery for handling and reducing ores, and the development of unexpectedly rich deposits.

In the Grass Valley mining district, the Empire mine with a recorded production of some $7 million in its 48 years of operation was supplementing its plant with the "most complete and best equipment of mining and milling machinery in the world."

The North Star, which had yielded over $6 million, continued to keep a 40-stamp mill busy.

The Allison Ranch, Omaha, W.Y.O.D., and Massachusetts Hill mines were also showing good prospects.

A new hoist and pumping plant, manufactured in Grass Valley by the Taylor Brothers foundry, was being installed in the Brunswick mine. Since the mine showed good prospects of developing into one of the biggest mines in the district, its stock almost doubled in value in a few months.

The Osborn Hill mine had been purchased by W. B. Bourn, Jr., the owner of the Empire mine. The mine was to be reopened with George W. Starr as the general manager and worked on a big scale by a company with ample capital backing.

In the Nevada City mining district, both the Providence and the Champion, which had produced more than $7 million each, were still going strong. Rich strikes had also been recently made at the New Texan and the Chapman ranch.

The biggest pump ever placed on a mine in Nevada County—if not in the state—was being constructed by the "wide-awake" foundrymen, the Taylor Brothers, for use at the Union Hill mine.

Interest in drift gravel mining at Nevada City was also "awakening."

In other local mining districts, the Delhi quartz mine at Columbia Hill had reopened, and the California mine in the Washington district was proving to be a bonanza.

The California Debris Commission was working on one of the most "stupendous engineering problems" ever contemplated in this section of the United States—the diversion of the entire flow of the Yuba River—so that hydraulic mining could be carried on without injuring agricultural interests and river navigation.

At the expenditure of more than $1 million, plans were being considered to divert the river into a canal that opened into a storage basin several miles wide and about 15 miles long that could receive hundreds of millions of cubic yards of debris from the hydraulic mines. The water was then to be returned to the Bear and Feather Rivers practically free from sediments.

Despite these grandiose plans, things were not going well for local hydraulic miners.

In July 1899, Sutter County had an injunction issued by the Superior Court to restrain the Red Dog Mining Company from dumping mining debris into Greenhorn Creek. The mine had been operating under a permit from the California Debris Commission.

A detective, unable to serve the court papers because he couldn't find all the owners, grumbled that every man, woman, and child, "almost," was acting as a spy in the interest of the miners to thwart him. He also declared that he had seen several hydraulic mines operating "full blast" tearing down immense banks with hydraulic monitors and washing the debris into Greenhorn Creek. He was afraid to approach the miners for fear they would turn their monitors on him.

In a meeting in San Francisco in July, the California State Miners' Association decided to back the Red Dog Mining Company in its defense and "exert every legal effort to have the Caminetti act declared unconstitutional." (The Caminetti Act allowed hydraulic mines to operate if their debris was kept out of streams and rivers and they were licensed by the California Debris Commission.)

In October 1899, the *Grass Valley Union* reported what it considered to be the greatest piece of mining news since the striking of the new "pay chute" in the old Empire that had led to the subsequent development of the Empire as one of the best mines in the state. The news was that an entirely new shoot of rich ore had been discovered on virgin ground in the old North Star mine. The discovery promised to revitalize the mine and make it as productive as ever.

Although mining prospects were the big news items throughout 1899 in Nevada County, progress was being made in several other areas.

The Nevada County Board of Supervisors had decided to build a new "neat but plain" jail that might cost as much as $25,000.

The Nevada County Electric Company, said to be the most complete on the Coast, had doubled its capacity and extended and improved its system to supply power to the mines for milling, hoisting, and pumping and to furnish 6000 lights to Nevada City and Grass Valley.

The Floriston Pulp and Paper Company was building the largest paper mill west of the Mississippi River 12 miles east of Truckee at Floriston. The plant, which would employ about 500 men, was to produce book, writing, manila, and tissue papers.

The ice industry in Truckee was flourishing, and the demand for Truckee lumber was increasing rapidly. Truckee mills had orders for 12,000,000 board feet of wood for orange boxes, a few million board feet for snowshed timbers, and 30,000 to 40,000 cords of wood for the new paper mill. Demands were also growing for timber for the Comstock mines, old and new railroads, old and new mine constructions, and rapidly expanding towns.

In Penn Valley, a large creamery was opened where local farmers could market their surplus milk.

A committee of Grass Valley trustees was contracting to have chuck holes in the streets improved, and the Grass Valley marshal was ordered to stop the Chinese from gardening on Colfax Avenue.

The number of new and elegant buildings going up in both Grass Valley and Nevada City proved that these cities were no longer just ordinary mining towns but were "solid, progressive" little cities that were increasing in "attractiveness and desirability."

More than a quarter million Woodpecker Cigars made by hand by well-paid skilled workers in Nevada City had been sold all over the state in 1898. The factory was the largest in Northern California and was believed to be "destined" to become one of the largest in the state.

Although the Bartlett pear production in the area was hurt by late frosts and hailstorms, local pears were in great demand because the mountain grown fruit had more sugar and flavor and better keeping qualities than valley pears.

A donkey steam engine hauling lumber at the King and Wolford sawmill in the early 1900s (Courtesy of Ardis Hatten Comstock).

The annual Donation Day parade in Grass Valley in the early 1900s (Courtesy of Harriet Jakobs).

Mr. Sanborn, a wholesale fruit buyer, expressed the opinion that there was little likelihood of an over-production of fruit in California and that growers in this area should be producing ten times their current quantity.

Growers were also being urged to experiment with planting vineyards and apple and peach orchards to make thousands of unimproved acres productive.

When the citizens of Nevada City overwhelmingly voted to accept bonds for the construction of a new sewer system, the *Grass Valley Union* predicted that in a few months there would be no more filth and slums in the "Queen City of the Sierra," which would help bring "desirable people to Nevada City" to spend their summer outings in this "balmy climate."

When the main line of the sewer system in Grass Valley was completed, the completion ceremony on Empire Street on Thanksgiving Day was witnessed by hundreds. A yellow flag was thrown into Wolf Creek to signify the "use of the yellow flag would be a thing of the past." (Yellow flags were nailed to doors to signify quarantines for infectious diseases, which were often spread by unsanitary conditions and contaminated water.)

During the ceremony, Mayor C. E. Clinch made a few "timely remarks," thanked the people for supporting the new sewer system, and expressed great hope for the future "healthfulness of Grass Valley." After Reverend E. R. Willis offered a brief prayer, the crowd went to Watt Park to see the baseball game.

The *Grass Valley Union* immediately urged everyone to keep their yards "perfectly clean" so Grass Valley could be one of the "foremost and cleanest cities in the state."

In February, when the boys who had volunteered to serve in the Spanish-American War returned to Nevada County, the whole county turned out to give them a hero's welcome home. The Eighth Regiment band from Marysville serenaded them from the balcony of the Holbrooke Hotel with patriotic and inspiring music. Main, Mill, and Church Streets were almost impassable when Company C of Nevada City led by the Grass Valley brass band marched by with their guns on their shoulders as a large crowd cheered and applauded.

In December, the 16th annual Donation Day in Grass Valley was greeted with enthusiasm and spirit as hundreds of school children and scores of business men and citizens marched up Main, down Mill, and up Neal to the Lincoln School building on School Street where their contributions of wood, potatoes, and sacks of flour and other "good things for the poor and unfortunate" were accepted by the "good ladies of the Relief Society."

But the greatest and most carefully planned Nevada County demonstration in 1899 was for the American Institute of Mining Engineers who visited the "Quartz Crowned Empress of the Sierra" in late September. Citizens were urged to do their "utmost to impress the guests" with the richness of the veins, the extensiveness of the mining industry, and the permanence of the mines in the area so the visitors could spread the word to investors and capitalists and give California mining the impetus needed for continued development.

The engineers and their wives were treated "right royally" as they were greeted at the Colfax station, conducted across the scenic narrow gauge route, made a stop along the way to tour the Brunswick mine, and were eventually lodged at hotels or in the homes "of the best people in the city."

In the afternoon, they were escorted in carriages and "carry-alls" to view the "grandest mines in the world." Most went "down the creek" where the Providence, Champion, Mountaineer, Home, Cadmus, Merrifield, Wyoming, and other mines were located in bunches on either side of Deer Creek. All kinds of refreshments, "liquid and solid," were served by a corps of local ladies.

Many went underground for the first time. In the mines, the shafts, drifts, and stopes were lighted with electric lights so no candles were necessary. Boards to walk on were also laid down so no one would soil their clothes.

In the evening, the visitors were serenaded by George's Band from the balcony of the Holbrooke Hotel before being served an elaborate banquet.

But all was not clean, light, and progressive throughout 1899 in Nevada County. Some old problems still plagued the area.

The Nevada City Board of Trustees was "seriously" talking about passing an ordinance prohibiting the playing of pianos and other musical instruments in saloons and resorts where liquor was sold and of removing the houses of "ill fame" from Spring Street.

Efforts by the *Grass Valley Union* to have Grass Valley saloons closed at midnight to help prevent drunken brawls and general disturbances of the peace was rejected because the majority of people signed a petition against such an ordinance.

At the Mayflower mine on Canada Hill, young Henry Hawk, the "powder monkey," and Samuel Bishop, a miner, were blown into "hundreds of fragments" when some giant powder exploded.

A rainstorm in March astonished even some of the old-timers. Bridges on Main and Broad Streets in Nevada City were crowded with spectators watching Deer Creek rage and boom with drift-wood and logs. A number of footbridges were washed away, and the sight of two vacant Chinese cabins that went floating down the

A typical barroom scene in the early 1900s.

Nevada City in the early 1900s (Courtesy of Bob Paine).

stream upset horses and riders. Old-timer A. Isoard agreed that the creek was high, but he also declared that it was a "good deal higher" when the old Jenny Lind Theatre was swept away in March 1852.

In March, nighwatchman William Kilroy was shot down in cold blood in Nevada City. Ed Moore—the "best roller skater" in the county and a dangerous character who had been in trouble before—was believed to be the killer. Moore was captured in Contra Costa County in April and subsequently tried, found guilty of murder, and sentenced to life imprisonment. Before leaving for prison, Moore gave his Lincoln quartz mine near Canada Hill to his lawyer, John R. Tyrrell.

Truckee's "601," which had become famous for cleaning the town of riff-raff at intervals, was revived to get rid of a crowd of "gamblers, cutthroats, fast women, and all kinds of objectionable characters" who had infested Truckee. A committee of 15 with pistols in hand toured all the saloons and other resorts and warned all those who were unwanted to leave town within 24 hours. Notices of—"This means you."—were also sent out. As a result, Truckee was once again a "simon-pure" town—for a time.

The morning stillness of the quiet town of Washington, 19 miles above Nevada City, was shattered by pistol shots when "passion-crazed" Louie Moreno shot and killed his paramour, Mrs. Lillie Riley, a "denizen of the tenderloin," and then shot and killed himself in front of the brothel.

Some plans for progress also hit a few bumps.

Penn Valley creamery.

When John F. Kidder announced that he would build an elaborate two-story, fire-proof, architecturally beautiful theater on his property on Bennett Street in Grass Valley, the *Grass Valley Union* praised the project as a monument to an enterprising, progressive man, who had done more than any other citizen in the city in making improvements and setting examples for others to follow.

When Captain John Cross of Los Angeles presented the idea of connecting Grass Valley and Nevada City with an electrical railroad—an idea that had been proposed and then dropped again and again in preceding years—the Board of Trustees of both cities were in favor of the proposal. However, J. F. Kidder—president of the Nevada County Narrow Gauge Railroad—immediately told the board members that he protested such a railroad, and if such a road were placed on Bennett Street, he would not spent another cent on any public improvements nor would he build a theater on Bennett Street or any other site.

The trustees decided to go ahead and advertise for a franchise for an electrical railroad, reasoning that Kidder could bid on the franchise along with anyone else interested.

Dr. Harris, a trustee of Grass Valley, further stated: "The progress of the city does not depend on any one man. This city will go on and on long after we are all in glory, shouting hallelujah."

Dr. Harris was right. Hallelujah!

About the Author

Juanita Kennedy Browne was born in Commerce and grew up in Picher, Oklahoma in the heart of a hard-rock lead and zinc mine district. She moved to California with her parents shortly after World War II where she worked for Douglas Aircraft in Long Beach and later for Aerojet-General in Sacramento. In 1972, she received her Master of Arts degree in English with a history minor from the California State University, Sacramento.

Juanita then began freelance writing. Although she has sold hundreds of articles on subjects ranging from aviation to zucchini to local, regional, and national newspapers and magazines, this is her first book.

In 1973 Juanita and her husband, Pete, and their two youngest boys, Juan and Dana, moved to their Christmas tree ranch in The Hollow in Grass Valley. Fascinated by the similarity between the hard-rock gold mines of the area and the mines of her home town, Juanita began mining the rich history she found in her new "backyard."

This book is a culmination of research that Juanita did for historical articles on Nevada County for various publications, for her monthly column on events 100 years ago in Nevada County that has been running for five years in the Grass Valley *Union,* and for radio spots on Nevada County history that she broadcasts for "home-town radio" KNCO each Wednesday.

References

For those who want to read more on any phase of California history, I would suggest they consult the extensive reference listings in *California Local History, A Bibliography and Union List of Library Holdings*, Second Edition, edited by Margaret Miller Rocq, published by the Stanford University Press, Stanford, California, in 1970 and the Supplement to the Second Edition that was published in 1976.

The Nevada County Libraries maintain pamphlet files of items on Nevada County history and also publish and periodically update a valuable reference listing of books on the general history of California, on gold mines and mining in California, and on directories, newspapers, census, periodicals, maps, and books on Nevada County history that are available through the Nevada County Library system.

Another invaluable source of articles, pamphlets, books, photographs, and records of all kinds is the holdings of the Searls Historical Library.

In my research for this book, I rummaged through all of these sources. I also browsed through that old standby *History of Nevada County, California* edited by Harry L. Wells and published by Thompson and West in 1880 and reprinted by Howell-North Books in 1970. That browsing, especially when looking for a specific person or event, became a "piece of cake" by using the Index to Thompson and West compiled by David A. Comstock and Ardis Hatten Comstock.

Two other excellent sources on California history written by excellent historians are:

California From the Conquest in 1846 to the Second Vigilance Committee in San Francisco by Josiah Royce, and

A Frontier Lady, Recollections of the Gold Rush and Early California by Sarah Royce.

These books are of particular significance to Nevada County history and historians because Josiah Royce was a genuine home-town boy who was born in Grass Valley on November 20, 1855. Years later, at Josiah's request, his mother, Sarah, wrote of her experience in crossing the plains to California in 1849. Other books on Nevada County history that I found useful were:

The Chicago Park Connection by Pat Jones,

Gold Cities, Grass Valley and Nevada City by Jim Morley and Doris Foley,

Gold Diggers and Camp Followers by David Allan Comstock,

Origins of Hydraulic Mining in California by Philip Ross May,

A Brief History of the Empire Mine at Grass Valley by Charles A. Bohakel, M.A.,

Fire and Ice, A Portrait of Truckee edited by Paul A. Lord, Jr.,

Truckee, An Illustrated History of the Town and Its Surroundings by Joanne Meschery,

Nevada County Narrow Gauge by Gerald M. Best,

The Divine Eccentric by Doris Foley,

Mines and Mineral Resources of Nevada County by the California State Mining Bureau,

One Hundred Years of Nevada County, 1851–1951 by the Nevada City Nugget,

Hydraulicking, A Brief History of Hydraulic Mining in Nevada County, California by Robert M. Wyckoff,

Give Me a Mountain Meadow: The Life of Charles Fayette McGlashan by M. Nona McGlashan, and

You Bet Gold Fever by Jerry Brady.

These books are intentionally not listed in any order, and I am not saying that all—or any—are "the best" sources on their particular subjects, but they do furnish information on phases of Nevada County history that is either relatively new or is not as widely available as other sources.

I also picked up good information by listening either to a friendly Park Ranger or docent while touring through the Marshall Gold Discovery State Historic Park, Malakoff State Historic Park, Empire Mine State Historic Park, and the Nevada County Historical Society's Firehouse No. 1 Museum in Nevada City and the North Star Mining Museum in Grass Valley.

Another source of information that I, as a member of the Nevada County Historical Society, would naturally refer to is the series of bulletins that have been published by the Society since 1948. The specific bulletins I used were: Vol. 1 No. 4; Vol. 3 Nos. 3 and 4; Vol. 5 Nos. 1, 2, and 5; Vol. 6 Nos. 1, 4, and 6; Vol. 7 No. 2; Vol. 8 No. 4; Vol. 10 Nos. 3 and 4; Vol. 12 No. 2; Vol. 13 Nos. 1 and 4; Vol. 14 No. 2; Vol. 15 Nos. 2 and 4; Vol. 16 No. 4; Vol. 17

Nos. 2 and 3; Vol. 18 No. 3; Vol. 19 No. 2; Vol. 20 Nos. 1 and 2; Vol. 23, No. 6; Vol. 27 No. 3; Vol. 30 Nos. 2, 3, and 4; Vol. 31 No. 2; Vol. 32 No. 4; Vol. 34 Nos. 3 and 4; Vol. 35 No. 3; and Vol. 37 No. 2.

Although these bulletins were written by many different people and therefore vary in style and accuracy, they do provide good historical leads on interesting subjects and general dates, names, and places.

I also did extensive research in all the Nevada County newspapers that are available for the period of 1853 through 1899. Many of the sections in the book are based on or verified by local newspaper reports. Much of the Truckee information was taken from files of the *Truckee Republican,* and all of the information in "Looking Forward and Backward—1899" came from the 1899 files of the *Grass Valley Daily Union.*

The information on Emma Nevada came mainly from files in the Searls Historical Library.

When I found disagreement among these sources, I selected—sometimes arbitrarily—the version that made the most sense to me or seemed to be the most widely accepted by seemingly "reputable" historians. I chose Knight rather than McKnight as the discoverer of gold on Gold Hill, and I decided to spell Attwood with two "t's" and Landsfeld with no "t," and to be consistent by not capitalizing the "m" in the name of any mine.

Also, if you have read the entire book, you have no doubt gathered that I have included material that is obviously more myth and legend than history. Again, I included these "dubious" data because I believe that even myth has a basis in fact—somewhere in some past time—and I did try to point out those stories that were just that—"stories"—and not necessarily valid history. I committed all these historical transgressions intentionally and happily because I enjoy those "stories" and I hope others will, too, for, in my opinion, history can be and should be enjoyable.

Nevada County Historical Society 1983

Board of Directors

President: Madelyn Helling.
Vice President: Bruce Bolinger.
Executive Secretary: Brita
  Rozynski.
Recording Secretary: Priscilla
  Kepfer.

Treasurer: Dorothy Graydon.
Museum Directors: Ed Tyson and
  Glenn Jones.
Publicity: Margaret Trivelpiece.
Publications: Peter van der Pas.
Liaison: Isabel Hefelfinger.

Directors: Charles Graydon, Charles Harrison, Cliff Sommarstrom, William Falconi, Dee Hatfield, Stuart Lott, Bill Wilbur, Wee Steuber, Constance Baer, and Juanita Browne.

Members

Ralph Achey
Phyllis O. Acker
George and JoAnn Aiello
Lucille D. Alexander
Herb Altman, Sr.
Violet Anders
Paul and Helen Anderson
Robert H. Austin
Juanita Avalos
Mrs. Constance Baer
Don Baird
Robert and Marguerite Baird
James A. Bale
Melinda Ballmer
Bancroft Library
Herbert E. Barker, Sr.
Barry R. Barnes
Olive Beck
Benjamin and Simone Becker
David Beesley and Family
Richard and Jane Bentley
Dorothy D. Berg
Dr. and Mrs. Hjalmer Berg
H. S. and Lorraine Bergtholdt
Dr. Elbridge J. Best

Gordon W. Betts
Kurt and Lori Billeter
Monroe and Julia Blaylock
Charles A. Bohakel
Bruce and Charlotte Bolinger
Jane Bollinger
Catherine Bonivert
Alice G. Borgnis
Ewald and Yvonne Bower
Marjorie Bozarth
Mrs. Hazel Bramkamp
Daniel L. Brennan
Gwynne Searls Brom
Scott R. Brooke
Elaine Brooksby
C. Merritt Brown
Ida C. Brown
Juanita and Pete Browne
Scott Browne
Frank H. Buck, Jr.
Lloyd E. Buell
Frances Burton
Phyllis Butz
Paul and Dorothy Byrne
Donna L. Cabral

William and Eileen Cain
George F. Cake
F. D. Calhoon
California State University,
  Sacramento
Jean W. Campbell
Anne M. Carlson
Herbert Carlson
James S. Carson
William and Blanche Casey
Terry M. Cassettari
Leonard and Bernice
  Chessman
Steve M. Chileski
Jack R. Chisholm
Victor and Pauline
  Christiansen
Mrs. Fidella Church
Robert Clapham
Bill and Laura Clark
Jack M. Clark
Ruth C. Clarke
Ludwig and Kathryn Clauset
Downey C. Clinch
Richard Allen Close

Howard and Joyce Cobb
Samuel W. Cocks
Stuart and Edwina Coffing
Alice E. Collins
Aubrey M. Commons
David and Ardis Comstock
Jack and Gay Conner
Mrs. Marian Conway
Glen and Nathalie Cooley
Aileen Cook
L. W. Coughlan
Shirley Coughlin
Miles D. Coughlin
Ruth J. Cramer
Nancy Fry Crane
Cecil L. Creech
Robert and Rena Culbertson
R. F. and Lois Cushing
Mary A. Danforth
Frances C. Davidson
Alan Davies
Lauren C. Davis
Bettie Decker
Estelle Deir
Frank G. Delfino
Charles and Sonja Delk
Richard and Phyllis DeMers
Hollis and Fran DeVines
Stan and Beryl Dick
William and Phyllis Dickerson
Alvin and Shirley Dilts
Jack and Starr Dinwiddie
Albert and Marilyn Dittmann
Michael W. Dobbins
Robert A. Dobbins
James and Pauline Dodds
Mrs. Arletta Douglas
Louise Dudley
Robert G. Dunlap
Justin and Jane Dyer
Lewis and Barbara Dymond
Evelyn Eden
Don and Gloria Beth Edwards
H. Dustin Eichler
Delores Eldridge
Susan Ellenbogen
Empire Mine Park Association
William and Lorretta Falconi
Tay Farley
Edward and Merle Fellersen
Joyce and Larry Ferguson
Bill and Norma Ferry
Joseph and Lois Figueira

Earl T. Fischer
Frank and Norma Fitzgerald
Elsie Flynn
Pete Forbes
Loiuse L. Frame
Christine Freeman
Richard and Patricia French
Wilma Friend
William E. Fuller
Edward E. Gant, Jr.
Kenneth Gardellis
Lewis and Jean Gardiner
Joe and Rose Gast
Bob and Thelma Gates
Terrence and Marguerite
   Genesy
Mario and Marguerite Gentili
Walter Gillen
Annette Gillett
Gary D. Gilley
Howard V. Golub
Warren and Jeanette
   Goodspeed
Sandra L. Goolsby
Ross and Maiya Gralia
Charles and Dorothy Graydon
Powell Greenland
Jean Gregory
Patricia Grieb
Dwight and Helen Griffin
Thomas D. Guzman
Mrs. Noweita Haisten
Malcolm and Elizabeth
   Hammill
Mary Hanley
Arlie and Sibley Hansen
Rich Hansen
Robert W. Hansen
Wyatt and Vivian Harris
Charles and Mary Harrison
John P. Hart
Steven Harte
Donald and Dee Hatfield
Caroline F. Heesche
Isabel Hefelfinger
Madelyn Helling
R. Arch and Edna Henry
Robert S. Heyser
James and Virginia Hickey
John R. Hilpert
Joseph C. Hinman, Jr.
Dr. Jim C. Hitchcock
Gordon and Jeannine Hodel

Beatrice Ott Hoge
Ruth E. Holub
Gyneth E. Hoover
Henry E. Huntington Library
Herbert and Marjorie Inskip
Benjamin and Allene Irwin
Lawrence Ivey
Frank and Harriet Jakobs
Helen Tick Jarkovsky
Boyd F. Johnson
Lavon M. Johnson
Barry and Phyllis Jones
E. W. and Frances Jones
Glenn and Pearl Jones
Pat and Buck Jones
Art and Betty Karnesky
Florence B. Keegan
Howard and Maybelle Keene
Helen Keisker
Margaret Kell
Priscilla Kepfer
Henrietta Kershaw
Oliver W. Kessler
Luvia Kilroy
William Kilroy
Muriel C. Kirksey
Noel W. Kirshenbaum
Hilmen Kjorlie
George Koenig
Theodore A. Kohler, Jr.
Dean and Patricia Kone
Rudolph W. Kopf
S. E. Koppel and Family
Miroslav Kovalcik
John Lee Koziar
Dr. Robert M. Kraft
Richard and Doris Laird
Donald and Vicki LaKatos
William H. Lambert
Donald and Geraldine Larson
Chester T. and Thekla Lasky
Margaret League
Elaine R. Legg
Royle and Dorothy Leighton
Antoinette Lenahan
Mr. and Mrs. John Lestelle
Will W. Lester
Sibyl L. Leuteneker
Ernest and Inez Lewis
Sally M. Lewis
Renee J. Lindke
Anthony and Jean Loughran
Dean and Marilyn Lloyd

Stuart and Rhea Lott
Mary V. Loughman
Mrs. Lawrie Lowden
Frank and Doris Mack
Marisa E. Maier
John and Helen Major
Edward J. Maloney
Sylvia Malott
Jerry A. Mann
Sandra C. Manning
Eileen Marcucci
Mario and Irene Maretti
Richard E. Markley
Harry A. Marnell
Joe M. Marshall
Mrs. Carl Maxwell
Gayle R. Mayfield
Harold and Luise McCullough
Jack W. McCurry
Mary E. McDaniel
June McIntosh
Walter and Carolyn McNabb
Arch and Margaret McPherson
John Hubert Mee, Jr.
Joyce Mehrkens
Dr. and Mrs. Keith Mercer
Cosa Mikiska
Angela Miller
Rebecca Miller
Frank and Florence Milliff
Allen Mitchum
Edward J. Mogler
Mary Montgomery
Alice W. Moody
Bruce Moore
Ric Moorhouse
Claire Morgan
Alonzo Moriel
Uvon C. Morley
Frank Morrish
Anita M. Morrison
Charles and Margery Morrison
L. Mueller
Wm. R. Murphy, M.D.
Darlene Musante
Gene W. Myers
Lyle and Sue Nadeau
Mrs. Howard Naffziger
Herman and Jacqueline Nash
Sandra Naylor
Gordon and Maralee
  Nelder-Adams
Judith W. Nelson

J. Edwin Nettell
Nancy M. Neudorfer
Nevada Union High School,
  Library
Nevada Union High School,
  Social Studies Department
Olive Newell
Tom Newmark
V. J. and Melba Nugent
Margaret and Russell Nygren
Norman Oates
Margaret O'Brien
Phyllis C. Ocker
Marvin Odom
Mrs. Leona Ohrt
John D. Olmsted
William and Kathy Osborn
Fritz and Frieda Oschbach
Donna Pack
Marian M. Padgett
Robert and Ruth Paine
C. M. Palmer
William L. Palmer
Wessley and Anita Paulsen
Charles and Elfreda Pardau
Dorothy C. Pardo
Robert and Jane Parker
Rhonda Pascoe
Doris M. Patrick
Elsie Peard
Harriet A. Pearce
Carol Pelayo
Mary Penberthy
Paul Perry
Eric and Ruth Peterson
Mary P. Pierce
Robert G. Pierce
John C. Pillsbury
William L. Pimentell
Grace M. Pinch
George and Sara Pink
Lillian A. Pinker
Bobbie and Henry Pitts
Pleasant Ridge School
Henry and Florine Plude
William R. Postell
Edwin T. Powell
Mildred Vail Quinn
Radio Systems Technology Inc.
John F. Rankin
H. E. and Patricia Rayner
Eunice E. Reader
Theo Reidt

Gilbert Richards
Joseph D. Richert
Beryl Robinson, Jr.
David and Beverly Robertson
Preston and Eleanor Roche
Robert E. Roesner
John T. and Thelma Ronan, Jr.
Gwen and Eric Rood
Bernard and Jeanette Rosen
Sarah T. Ross
Brita and Roman Rozynski
Thomas and Paulette Rudolph
Joe W. Ruess
Edward and Marjorie Sample
S. M. Sanor
Elizabeth A. Santos
Donald R. Schmidt
Elizabeth Schmoyer
Wayne and Viola Scoles
Gordon and Karen Seagraves
Fred and Doris Searls
Berniece Selaya
Seven Hills School, Library
Marian Uphoff Sevier
Sandie J. Shaver
Charles M. Shaw
Maude Shaw Antiques
Ronald and Barbara Shaw
Raymond E. Shine
Mr. and Mrs. Burrell Shirey
Jack F. Siegfried
Neal and JoAnn Silence
J. A. Simmons
Manila May Skibinski
John and Ruth Skoverski
Paul and Shirley Slavonic
Grace I. Slyter
Gail L. Smart
Charles and Winabeth Smith
Bessie H. Smyth
Clifford and Nancy
  Sommarstrom
Mr. and Mrs. D. Sommer
Bradley and Renee Sonderman
Willard Wayne Sorensen
Robert and Nadine Southern
Jane L. Speed
Floyd and Virginia Sphar
Margaret M. Squaires
Dorothy J. Standish
Stanford University, Green
  Library
Marilyn Starkey

Charles and Ann Steinfeld
Mrs. Alwildia Steuber
John Steuber
Mrs. Elsar E. Stevens
Lloyd Stevenson
George and Margaret Stewart
Peter C. Stofle
Mack Stoker
Mr. and Mrs. Hamilton Stone
Chris and Fran Stritzinger
Florence Styles
Irene C. Suess
Maxine and Kevin Taylor
Charmayne Tellez
Charlene Thomas
Isabell M. Thomas
Lila L. Thomas
Lorene Thomas
Mary Thomas
Daniel and Donna Thuet

John E. Tremewan
Margaret Trivelpiece
Albert Troost
Kim S. Truro
Mrs. Hope Tryce
Osmer and Mary Tucker
Troy Tuggle
Edwin Tyson
Donald E. Underwood
Peter and Mary van der Pas
Frances W. Von Ahnen
Rena M. Walker
Gordon L. Wall
Larry and Gloria Walsh
Lew Wanamake
Donald E. Wangberg
James Wangberg
John and Audrey Weills
Ellis R. Weisker
Wells Fargo Bank, History
    Room

John and Loretta White
Gene and Alice Williams
Pauline Whiting
William and Violet Wilbur
Dale and Virginia Williams
Beth Wilson
Jacquelyn F. Wilson
Wisconsin State Historical
    Society
Susan J. Wolbarst
Vivian Wood
John Woolman School
Jean H. Worthington
Edward and Margaret Wright
Grace Wulf
Chet Yarber
Yuba County Library
Jerry and Patricia Zarriello
Claude and Mildred Zigler

Index

This book was designed by Juanita and Pete Browne in
collaboration with Dave Comstock.
Composition by Dwan Typography of Nevada City, California.
Printing by Blue Dolphin Press of Grass Valley, California.